Our Bishops, Heroes for the New Evangelization

Our Bishops, Heroes for the New Evangelization
Faithful Shepherds and the Promotion of Lay Doctrinal Literacy

Justin McClain

WIPF & STOCK · Eugene, Oregon

OUR BISHOPS, HEROES FOR THE NEW EVANGELIZATION
Faithful Shepherds and the Promotion of Lay Doctrinal Literacy

Copyright © 2017 Justin McClain. All rights reserved. Except for brief quotations in critical publications or reviews, no part of this book may be reproduced in any manner without prior written permission from the publisher. Write: Permissions, Wipf and Stock Publishers, 199 W. 8th Ave., Suite 3, Eugene, OR 97401.

Wipf & Stock
An Imprint of Wipf and Stock Publishers
199 W. 8th Ave., Suite 3
Eugene, OR 97401

www.wipfandstock.com

PAPERBACK ISBN: 978-1-4982-8422-6
HARDCOVER ISBN: 978-1-4982-8424-0
EBOOK ISBN: 978-1-4982-8423-3

Manufactured in the U.S.A.   MAY 4, 2017

Dedication

2015, when I began writing this book, was a remarkable year for the global episcopate, to whom this book is dedicated. As such, in conjunction with the World Meeting of Families in September 2015 (which coincided with the first visit of Pope Francis to the United States during his pontificate), the Ordinary Synod of Bishops on the Family in October 2015 (which came a year after the Extraordinary Synod of Bishops on the Family in October 2014), the fiftieth anniversary of Vatican II's *Christus Dominus: Decree Concerning the Pastoral Office of Bishops in the Church* (proclaimed on October 28, 1965), the two hundredth memorial of the death of Archbishop John Carroll (the first American bishop) on December 3, 1815, as well as in memory of the tenth anniversary of the conclusion of Saint John Paul II's pontificate and his subsequent journey toward the beatific vision on April 2, 2005, this work is dedicated to all of our faithful Catholic bishops throughout the world. Thank you for your tirelessly pastoral Christian ministry. We, your global congregation, offer our due gratitude. Your selfless love for Jesus Christ and the church have ultimately given greater glory to the kingdom of God, whose "light shines in the darkness, and the darkness has not overcome it" (John 1:5).

"For lack of guidance, a people falls;
security lies in many counselors."

(Prov 11:14)

"If one yearns for wide experience,
[wisdom] knows the things of old,
and infers the things to come."

(Wis 8:8)

"Spurn not the discourse of the wise,
but acquaint yourself with their proverbs;
from them you will acquire the training
to serve in the presence of princes.
Reject not the tradition of old men
which they have learned from their fathers;
from it, you will obtain the knowledge
how to answer in time of need."

(Sir 8:8–9)

Contents

Preface | *ix*
Acknowledgments | *xiii*
Introduction: "Upon this Rock" | *xv*

1 Catholic Education: Passing on the Light of Faith | 1
2 The Deposit of Faith: Honoring Sacred Scripture and Sacred Tradition | 9
3 Ecology and Environmental Custody: Respecting God's Creation | 17
4 Ecumenism and Interreligious Dialogue: Striving for God's Will, Striving for Good Will | 26
5 Evangelization: The Good News of Christ is Ever New | 35
6 Human Sexuality: Treasuring God's Remarkable Plan | 43
7 Immigrants and Refugees: Recognizing Our Brethren | 52
8 International Relations: Healing a Broken World | 60
9 The Laity and the Universal Call to Holiness: Understanding the Post-Vatican II Dynamic | 68
10 Marriage, the Family, and the Gift of Children: Promoting a Sacred Institution and the Foundation of Society | 76
11 Persecution of the Global Church: Living as "Sheep in the Midst of Wolves" | 84

CONTENTS

12 The Poor and Vulnerable: Serving Christ in Our Midst | 92
13 The Public Square and the Church: Complementing, Not Excluding | 101
14 Racial and Ethnic Harmony: Restoring and Promoting Societal Accord | 110
15 Sanctity of Human Life: Celebrating the First and Ultimate of All Rights | 118
16 A Conclusive Message of Gratitude for Our Bishops | 128

About the Author | *137*
Bibliography | *139*

Preface

In his 2009 book *Men of Brave Heart: The Virtue of Courage in the Priestly Life*, Archbishop José Gómez, then of the Archdiocese of San Antonio and now of the Archdiocese of Los Angeles, wrote the following regarding all Catholics' *universal call to holiness* within chapter 1, *The Beginning of Strong Courage: The Virtues, the Priesthood, and the New Evangelization of America*: "The universal call to holiness is the call that Christ makes to sinners—to all of us, clergy, religious, and laity alike—to repent and believe in the Gospel. Christ did not imagine a one-time conversion. Every Christian life, even the life of the priest, is a life of daily conversion. It is a lifelong process by which we try daily to more and more conform our lives to Christ and to his teaching."[1] Although Archbishop Gómez intended *Men of Brave Heart* essentially for his fellow priests, his words remind us that Christ's call for us to learn more and more about the will of God is an expectation that every Catholic should take seriously. This is particularly relevant when we consider the unique magisterial teaching role held by bishops, such as Archbishop Gómez, as they lead and guide their flock to Christ. As such, this book is primarily intended for the laity, but it is likewise intended for Catholics within any vocation who are

---

1. Gómez, *Men of Brave Heart*, 26.

desiring to learn more about the heroically pastoral writings of our faithful Catholic bishops.

It would hardly be possible to compress, or even summarize, nearly two thousand years' worth of bishops' writings into one documentary volume. There are far too many sources available, and even a lifetime would not reasonably afford such an endeavor. However, the reality that there are so many sources at hand should be conceived as a strength indicative of the church's unity, rather than as a burden of literary proportions. This is not to mention that to bring about such a project in printed form would most likely grossly violate the rhetorical trajectory of my chapter on the bishops' theological treatment of ecological matters. As such, this work is intended to merely provide a sampling of the myriad manners in which the bishops have charitably and accurately presented the truths of the Gospel since the time of Christ's earthly ministry, when he instituted the church. Therefore, rather than even aspiring to be summative or evaluative, this book is more *exemplary* (in the veritable sense of the term) in its scope. It is not conceptualized as any semblance of a moral treatise, because our bishops and numerous other orthodoxy-propounding moral theologians have repeatedly and successfully underscored the critical elements of Catholic social teaching throughout various epochs imbued with pertinent ecclesial activity.

Just as it would be a tribulation to mention and address all of the available texts, so too would it be a dire challenge to include the contributions of most, let alone all, of our Catholic bishops. As such, the exclusion of the mention of any particular prelate from around the world is, in no way, intended to devalue his contributions to the church; rather, this book seeks to highlight the unitive nature of the truth of the Lord by highlighting various bishops' efforts to maintain the continuity of evangelization throughout the ages, in accord with Jesus' Great Commission to his Apostles prior to his Ascension, which forms the conclusion of Matthew's Gospel, the great "teaching" Gospel: "Go, therefore, and make disciples of all nations, baptizing them in the name of the Father, and of the

Son, and of the Holy Spirit, teaching them to observe all that I have commanded you" (Matt 28:19–20a).

In effect, this book will hopefully serve as a measure of encouragement for the faithful to read more of the bishops' writings, in order to achieve an even fuller comprehension and fluency when it comes to intellectually concretizing and sharing the foundational elements of the faith, for purposes of catechesis, personal devotion, additional scholarly endeavors, or otherwise. Admittedly, and purposefully, there is a noticeable presence of (as opposed to a total reliance on) the written contributions of American bishops, for a couple of key reasons: the immediate availability of their untranslated writings, particularly in book form, for the English-speaking world, which is currently the readership of this book, as well as the diversity of American bishops in terms of their condition as a cross-section of a very culturally diverse American landscape with varying (not to be confused with *divergent*) theological approaches that still manage to provide an accurate presentation of Gospel-infused ecclesial principles.

At times, documents issued by episcopal committees, e.g. the United States Conference of Catholic Bishops, rather than individual prelates, will be addressed. However, the offerings of bishops from around the world will, of course, be offered, especially given that the popes throughout the millennia have come from other geographic locations. Yet another point to consider is that there is a focus on writings by prelates of the twentieth and twenty-first centuries, principally since they reiterated prior writings based on realities of former eras. Such literary formats as papal encyclicals, apostolic exhortations, pastoral letters, council documents, and published books will be used to exemplify our bishops' contributions to guiding the laity within the Catholic Church. Where pertinent, excerpts will appear from the current versions of the laity-accessible *New American Bible* and *Catechism of the Catholic Church*.

Given that we are in the "Digital Age," coupled with the celebratory nature of widespread literacy, it would present a challenge to posit that the faithful do not have practically instant access to the written contributions of the bishops, our models of Christian fidelity. A final note has to do with the fair question of why I have written this book—essentially, given that I am a member of the laity (a married father of children whom my wife and I hold to be precious gifts from God), my lack of status as a member of the clergy, let alone the episcopate, has provided me with the wherewithal to express appreciation for our Catholic bishops without running the risk of implying any pretentions of hierarchical ambition or bias; in other words, I have nothing to gain in ecclesial regard. Rather, this book is merely an opportunity to give back to those who have given so much to the church, who are our bishops: Christians, shepherds, heroes for the New Evangelization.

Acknowledgments

Foremost, thank you to my wonderful wife Bernadette for your supreme patience and support while I undertook this daunting, but grace-filled, project. You and the kids are my inspiration, and I love you with all my heart. Thank you to my brother Jaris and sister-in-law Lauren, a faithful Catholic couple worthy of emulation, for looking over the chapters on ecumenism and interreligious dialogue, international relations, and persecution of the global church (Jaris) and racial and ethnic harmony (Lauren). Thank you to my helpful colleagues at Bishop McNamara High School. Thank you to my fellow BMHS theology teacher and dear friend Nancy Cunningham for reviewing the chapter on marriage, the family, and the gift of children. Thank you to fellow BMHS theologian Hunter Gallagher for reviewing my chapters on human sexuality, as well as the laity and the universal call to holiness. Thank you to my BMHS theologian colleague Martin Hipkins, a full-time theology teacher by day and a busy law school student by night (not to mention a new husband and father), for sacrificing your precious time and energy to examine and critique my chapter on the public square and the church, and also for providing the resourceful publication on some of John Paul II's *ad limina* addresses to the American bishops. Thank you to BMHS biology and environmental science teacher Jan Steeger, a faithful Catholic and

Acknowledgments

member of the Archdiocese of Washington's Caring for Creation Committee, for reviewing my chapter on ecology and environmental custody. Thank you to Michael Amodei, a family man and executive editor of Adolescent Catechesis at Ave Maria Press, likewise an author extraordinaire and the University of Notre Dame's #1 fan, who somehow manages to find time to offer experience-riddled feedback and insights while simultaneously recalling the history and statistics for nearly every college and professional athletic team in American history. Thank you to Tonya Bubolz, a truly caring person and experienced theology teacher, for your input on the chapters on evangelization and on the sanctity of human life. Thank you to my good friend Dr. Ray Fermo for your keen eye while reading through the chapters on how the bishops have aided immigrants and refugees, as well as the poor and vulnerable. Thank you to the editorial staff at Wipf and Stock Publishers, who have offered their highly respected recommendations and expertise in making this endeavor a reality. Thank you to our Catholic bishops for your reliably courageous Christian witness, even in the face of numerous challenging pastoral considerations. Lastly, and most vitally, thank God for having given humanity a chance.

Introduction
"Upon this Rock"

"And so I say to you, you are Peter, and upon this rock I will build my Church, and the gates of the netherworld shall not prevail against it."

(MATT 16:18)

In January 2015, a crowd of between six and seven million people convened in the Philippine capital of Manila. They were not there for a concert, an inauguration, or a coronation. They were there to celebrate the Eucharist to be consecrated by a bishop, Pope Francis, the successor of Saint Peter. Twenty years earlier, [Saint] Pope John Paul II had drawn a similarly immense crowd of four to five million faithful. In each scenario, the crowd had come to listen to the words of the vicar of Christ. In each setting, the crowd had come to the pope, and the pope had come to the crowd. A shepherd and his flock were together, with the latter in the former's care.

A pope and his fellow bishops have the responsibility of imitating Jesus, the Good Shepherd (see John 10:1–21). It is no wonder that Christian typology from the Old Testament exhibits that such covenantal figures as Moses and David were, themselves, shepherds (see Exod 3:1 and 1 Sam 17:20, 34–37, respectively). In the New Testament, the Gospel of Luke shows us that the shepherds, although they were the lowliest in society, were the first to learn of Christ's birth (see Luke 2:8–20). The imagery of a shepherd and his flock is clear—the shepherd not only defends, shelters, and feeds his sheep, but he likewise "[goes] after the lost one until he finds it" (Luke 15:4). Since Jesus' institution of the church and the accompanying papacy (see Matt 16:18), apostolic succession has provided the church with an unbroken line of popes and their bishops who have patiently, dutifully, and charitably shepherded their flock for the furtherance of the kingdom of God. This is a point that we will return to imminently, following an extensive, but relevant, personal aside.

Regarding church history specifically and all of human history broadly, history has a certain potent mystique. Even those who are not professional historians or are opponents of the soporific effects of historical documentaries tend to have at least a modicum of respect for the idea of the journey of our ancestors who preceded us in humanity, along with their accompanying experiences throughout innumerable millennia. Hence, as a high school theology teacher, one of my favorite kernels of knowledge to impart on my students is that one of the many dilemmas with making blanket statements evaluating the too frequently occurring term "biblical times" is that, essentially, roughly the same amount of time passed between Abraham's earthly life and Jesus' earthly life as between Jesus' earthly life and our own earthly lives (nearly two thousand years from 1,900 BC to 6–4 BC [taking into account adjusted dating] and just over two thousand years from 6–4 BC to today, respectively). As such, chronologically speaking, Jesus' Incarnation is a relatively recent feature of our humanity broadly, as well as salvation history particularly. Notwithstanding how recently Jesus walked the earth, the average person, Christian or otherwise, who values history at least to a marginal extent, would appreciate the theological or anthropological concept of a constant sequence of contact between modern times and when Jesus walked the earth.

Introduction

I rarely extend extra credit opportunities to my students. However, on those infrequent occasions when I do, I aim to make the assignment as pedagogically worthwhile as possible. One such occasion came after I announced to my theology students that I would be offering them extra credit if they attended a special mass on Sunday, May 18, 2014, at Sacred Heart Church, a parish of the Archdiocese of Washington located in Bowie, Maryland. The mass was in celebration of the 225th anniversary of the election of Archbishop John Carroll as the first Catholic bishop of the United States on May 18, 1789. Archbishop Carroll was chosen by his fellow Jesuits in the old chapel on the since-expanded grounds of Sacred Heart Church, and his name was submitted to the Vatican and approved by Pope Pius VI later that same year. The United States had its first pastor for the original thirteen colonies.

Coincidentally, my wife, our children, and I are parishioners at Sacred Heart, so we were present at the same mass, and I was gratified to see how many of my students took advantage of the extra credit opportunity. (I told them that I would be there, so apparently, the idea of running into their teacher outside of school on the weekend was not a sufficiently deterrent prospect to inspire their reclusion.) As part of the students' extra credit assignment, they had to pay close attention to the words of the principal celebrant, Cardinal Donald Wuerl of the Archdiocese of Washington, during his homily. I was unaware of what Cardinal Wuerl would discuss, but I safely surmised that it would relate to the contributions of Archbishop Carroll to the Catholic Church locally, regionally, nationally, and globally: ultimately, *universally*.

Returning to the topic of the reality of a link to the person of Christ himself—fully God and fully man—within history, I found myself intrigued by what Cardinal Wuerl shared in his homily regarding an encounter that he once had with an inquisitive young child one day after mass. As the boy stood with his parents, looking up at Cardinal Wuerl, the boy was fascinated to learn that Cardinal Wuerl was part of a continuous line of shepherds who, if observed over the course of the past two thousand years, extended all the way back to Jesus' closest followers, the Apostles. This apostolic

Introduction

succession, referenced earlier, connects Saint Peter directly to Pope Francis, and thereby tangibly extends its theological scope back in history to the very person of Jesus Christ.

What is contained in the following chapters is a thematic exposition of some of the many circumstances through which our bishops have, through the guidance of the Holy Spirit, so faithfully and heroically inspired their congregations around the globe to be drawn to the person of Jesus Christ. Over the course of approximately two thousand years thus far, the steady march of this unbroken line of apostolic succession has been frequently tumultuous, occasionally dramatic, painstakingly documented, and hardly inconsequential. However, as more than an elementary overview of specific instances of pastoral heroism, this book essentially serves as a call to the faithful to closely heed the advice, whether through admonition or praise, of our bishops throughout the world. Similarly, it is a measure of gratitude to our shepherds for the care that they have bestowed upon their sheep. One of my students once asked me: "Do bishops get lonely?" This was a concise, yet fair, quip that drew me to ponder the question's greater implication. What we can securely conclude is that, with a supportive congregation, whether in their assigned diocese, administrative position, or similar ecclesial post, our bishops can rest in the peace of knowing that they are in the company of a faithful flock who is attentive to their call to follow Christ as we all strive to live the "universal call to holiness in the Church"[1] highlighted in chapter 5 of *Lumen Gentium*, the Vatican II dogmatic constitution on the church, and such a call surely undergirds the Good News of Jesus Christ.

---

1. Paul VI, *Lumen Gentium*, 39–42.

1

Catholic Education
Passing on the Light of Faith

"Train the young in the way they should go;
even when old, they will not swerve from it."
(Prov 22:6)

Throughout the nearly two thousand year history of the Catholic Church, Catholic education has come in a variety of forms. These include tutorial arrangements, as were provided to the children of nobility—especially in areas of Europe and Asia—well beyond the Middle Ages, the traditional classroom, which is practically as old, homeschooling, and other settings, which are increasingly innovative as we advance through the twenty-first century. In fact, at this stage of educational history, various Catholic educational institutions have even begun to offer courses through distance learning (typically via the Internet), from the level of elementary school through doctoral studies.

No matter the pedagogical structure of the Catholic educational system at hand, the goal should be the same—availing platforms that facilitate not only learning per se, but learning that is oriented toward opportunities to serve the kingdom of God. Just as bishops of past generations have done, our modern-day bishops have been influential proponents of Catholic education. As we continue into the twenty-first century, our bishops' dynamic promotion of Catholic education will further permit Catholic schools, from K-12 through higher education, to live out their privileged mission of proclaiming the Good News to broader society.

An important starting point when it comes to gaining an understanding of the role of Catholic education within society is the Vatican II document *Gravissimum Educationis: Declaration on Christian Education*. Although this document is from 1965, over fifty years ago, its implications for Catholic education are just as valid in the twenty-first century world. For example, one can consider "the remarkable development of technology and scientific investigation and the new means of communication"[1] just as valid two decades into the twenty-first century as they were in the mid-1960s. At the core of Catholic education rests the expectation that students be drawn to "a deeper knowledge and love of God."[2] If this endeavor is not in place, students will not have the same opportunity to prosper spiritually to an enduring extent, and society will subsequently not be as enriched with the presence of charity, which can never be taken for granted.

Catholic Identity in an Educational Context

An important way in which bishops have furthered the mission of Catholic schools is by encouraging an embrace of Catholic identity. *Catholic identity* is admittedly one of those terms that is easier to *recognize* than to *define*. When a Catholic school has a robust and vigorous atmosphere of Catholicity at its core, rather than being a mirage of Gospel-centered values, it is then carrying out the true mission of Catholic education in regard to encouraging students to bring Christ into the world. Thus, to speak of Catholic identity

---

1. Paul VI, *Gravissimum Educationis*, Introduction.
2. Ibid., 1.

signifies ensuring that the curriculum is centered on Catholic values, including the church's moral teachings, lest students be led astray. Indeed, it is rational to concede that, as Cardinal Wuerl emphasizes in his 2011 book *Seek First the Kingdom: Challenging the Culture by Living Our Faith*, regarding what has occurred in optimum realms throughout the history of Catholic education: "Catholic education would be reflected not only in the classroom, but also in campus life. Theology would be given an honored place in the curriculum, supreme among the sciences."[3] Similarly, in his October 2016 pastoral letter *The Future of Our Catholic Schools*, Bishop Philip Egan of the Diocese of Portsmouth, United Kingdom, notes: "In a Catholic school—independent, voluntary aided, free, or academy—everything should be done to create an authentic Christian ethos."[4]

Further regarding Catholic identity, as the bishops have reminded us, it is critical for the laity—both within and outside of Catholic educational systems—to fathom that Catholic education is the most effective in drawing students closer to Christ when it reinforces the positive values that the student is ideally already acquiring at home: "The family which has the primary duty of imparting education needs help of the whole community."[5] As Archbishop William Lori of Baltimore notes in his 2015 book *The Joy of Believing: A Practical Guide to the Catholic Faith*: "In the family, children learn life's most basic lessons, including how to respect and love one another, how to tell the truth, and how to grow in virtue."[6]

The bishops have emphasized that to provide a framework of strong Catholic identity does not somehow imply shielding students from "the world"; rather, it more properly forms them in terms of how to spread the Gospel within the world. *Gravissimum Educationis*, even fifty years ago, spoke of "the pluralism that exists

---

3. Wuerl, *Seek First the Kingdom*, 134.
4. Egan, *The Future of Our Catholic Schools*, 2.
5. Paul VI, *Gravissimum Educationis*, 3.
6. Lori, *The Joy of Believing*, 166–67.

today in ever so many societies,"[7] thereafter referring to "the pluralism of contemporary society."[8] In the milieu of these pluralistic realities, as addressed in terms of ecumenism and interreligious dialogue particularly, Catholic schools must prepare students to engage with the world by focusing on reflecting an array of curricular considerations, "but especially the moral education it must impart."[9] Thus, as Catholic bishops have reinforced over the course of generations, those professionals tasked with imparting Catholic education can hardly hope to be contributing to the kingdom of God by permitting the teaching of that which is held to be morally objectionable, in light of the church's wisdom-laden experience and subsequently seasoned doctrinal and dogmatic teachings.

For decades, the bishops have emphasized that readily noticeable Catholic identity benefits those students of other faith traditions who attend Catholic educational institutions. *Gravissimum Educationis* mentions that "the Church must be present with her own special affection and help for the great number who are being trained in schools that are not Catholic,"[10] and "the Church considers very dear to her heart those Catholic schools, found especially in areas of the new churches, which are attended also by students who are not Catholics."[11] In his 2008 pastoral letter, *Catholic Education: Looking to the Future with Confidence*, Cardinal Wuerl notes briefly, yet cogently, that, "[w]hile our schools are Catholic and present a vision of life inspired by Jesus, many of the students are not Catholic. They come because our schools work."[12] On a final note regarding dialogue with those of other faith traditions, Nigerian Cardinal Francis Arinze, in his 1998 book *Meeting Other Believers: The Risks and Rewards of Interreligious Dialogue*, while not addressing the identity of Catholic schools per se in this instance, makes a key point that is not unrelated to the expectation

---

7. Paul VI, *Gravissimum Educationis*, 6.
8. Ibid., 7.
9. Ibid., 6.
10. Ibid., 7.
11. Ibid., 9.
12. Wuerl, *Catholic Education*, 16.

of Catholic schools to underscore their affinity for the church and her teachings:

> Christians who, while engaged in interreligious dialogue, would like to hide their Christian identity, or at least to de-emphasize it, seem to be saying, without words, that Christ is an obstacle or an embarrassment to dialogue, and that they have found a better formula for contact with others that consists in setting aside for the moment that they are sent by Christ. To state the situation in these terms is to show that an authentic Christian should not adopt such a stance. As Christians, we should realize and recognize who we are and to whom we are witnesses. Only then can we be good ambassadors of the Christian faith community. And if we are Catholics, we should not hide this when we meet others. We do not promote dialogue authentically by suppressing our religious identity.[13]

Catholic Education at Various Levels

When endeavoring to consider the extensive breadth of bishops' support of Catholic education, it is necessary to examine Catholic education in its multi-faceted contexts. What constitutes Catholic education between multiple levels? When we think *Catholic education*, we tend to consider this in terms of K-12. In his pastoral letter *Catholic Education*, Cardinal Wuerl mentions: "In our Catholic elementary and secondary schools, parish religious education programs, adult faith formation, the Rite of Christian Initiation of Adults, sacramental formation programs, and the many forms of youth ministry, campus ministry, and evangelizing research, the threads of the encounter with Christ and his life-giving message are woven into the fabric of our human experience."[14] Thus, Catholic education is in place prior to kindergarten, as well as beyond

---

13. Arinze, *Meeting Other Believers*, 44–45.
14. Wuerl, *Catholic Education*, 5.

the post-secondary level. At all levels of Catholic education, homeschooling is likewise a noteworthy setting.

Looking at the United States specifically, according to Georgetown University's Center for Applied Research in the Apostolate ("CARA"—one of the most reliable sources of data for statistics related to the state of the church in the United States), as of 2016, there were 1,340,000 students in 5,266 Catholic elementary schools, 578,477 students in 1,212 Catholic high schools, and 776,443 students in 221 Catholic colleges and universities.[15] Delineating the role of the various levels of Catholic education, *Gravissimum Educationis* makes direct reference to "primary and secondary schools, the foundation of education,"[16] indicating that these two levels in particular are those that are substantively formative in terms of preparing students to later solidify, reinforce, and synthesize their knowledge through higher education.

Higher education deserves its own particular treatment, not the least reason being the role that the Catholic Church had in formulating the first universities, including such internationally renowned institutions as the Universities of Bologna, Italy (1088), Oxford, England (1096), Salamanca, Spain (1134), Paris, France (1150), Cambridge, England (1209), and others. As Cardinal Wuerl reminds us in *Seek First the Kingdom*, "[t]he secular university system, as we know it today, is actually a product of the medieval Church, which established its schools (for example, the University of Paris) to train theologians and clergy."[17] Cardinal Wuerl goes on to remind us that, "[a] Catholic university should be an academic center where the faith permeates the culture."[18] Fortunately, papal documents such as Saint Pope John Paul II's apostolic constitution *Ex Corde Ecclesiae: On Catholic Universities* remind us of the critical role that educators in Catholic universities worldwide have in professing the eternal truths of Christ. Indeed, as Saint John Paul

---

15. CARA, "Frequently Requested Church Statistics."
16. Paul VI, *Gravissimum Educationis*, 9.
17. Wuerl, *Seek First the Kingdom*, 132.
18. Ibid., 134.

II offers, "[i]t is the honor and responsibility of a Catholic university to consecrate itself without reserve to *the cause of truth*."[19]

Homeschooling plays a significant role in society as far as the ultimate goals of Catholic education are concerned. Unfortunately, there occasionally arise not only myths and misperceptions about different categories of how to best educate children, but likewise the perception of an adversarial mentality between Catholic educational institutions and homeschooling settings, for more reasons than can adequately be addressed in this book. Different educational settings need not be opposed, especially when the ultimate goal is to provide students with an educational atmosphere that is most conducive to laboring to get them into heaven while challenging them academically so that they can go out to make the world more reflective of the kingdom of God: "to foster a sense of values, to prepare for professional life."[20] In effect, the gifts offered by different school settings that have arisen throughout church history, including homeschooling and similar inter-personal tutorial curricular frameworks, have much to contribute to each other. As one example among various, classical school settings have made great strides in preparing twenty-first century leaders who are able to integrate and accurately impart the faith.

No matter the school setting, the laity must join the bishops in recalling parents' noble role concerning educating their children: "Since parents have given children their life, they are bound by the most serious obligation to educate their offspring and therefore must be recognized as the primary and principal educators. This role is so important that only with difficulty can it be supplied where it is lacking."[21] As such, returning to the topic of how all Catholic educational frameworks in all circumstances are called to engage with the broader community, "the family is the first school of the social virtues that every society needs."[22]

---

19. John Paul II, *Ex Corde Ecclesiae*, 4.
20. Paul VI, *Gravissimum Educationis*, 5.
21. Ibid., 3.
22. Ibid.

Hope for the Future of Catholic Education

As we continue into the twenty-first century, we would do well to support the bishops' reminders regarding the future of Catholic education, taking ever more seriously such considerations as "the latest advances in psychology and the arts and science of teaching,"[23] with "continuing readiness to renew and to adapt,"[24] "with a pedagogical skill that is in keeping with the findings of the contemporary world."[25] In his 2014 pastoral letter, *Equipping Saints: A Pastoral Letter on Catholic Education and Faith Formation*, Archbishop Charles Chaput, O.F.M. Cap., of Philadelphia provides no small charge to those tasked with educating the youth: "Our teachers and catechists remain the most influential models of Christian living our students encounter outside of the family,"[26] and this is not to mention the sobering expectation that "Catholic education is about making saints; about growing the seeds of *virtue and truth*. Anything less cheats our students of their dignity."[27] Fortunately, when it comes to teaching itself, the Catholic faithful have a model in the bishops, themselves shepherds called to imitate Jesus, the Good Shepherd, as Archbishop Lori reminds us in *The Joy of Believing*: "By teaching, together with priests, bishops lead people to explicit faith, to the sacraments, and to obedience to Christ's commandment of love."[28]

---

23. Ibid., 1.
24. Ibid., 5.
25. Ibid., 8.
26. Chaput, *Equipping Saints*, 3.
27. Ibid., 7.
28. Lori, *The Joy of Believing*, 99.

2

The Deposit of Faith
Honoring Sacred Scripture and Sacred Tradition

"All scripture is inspired by God and is useful for teaching, for refutation, for correction, and for training in righteousness, so that one who belongs to God may be competent, equipped for every good work."

(2 Tim 3:16–17)

The contributions of bishops when it comes to guarding the deposit of faith—sacred scripture and sacred tradition—over the course of nearly two millennia could hardly be overstated. Examining the particular period from the end of the nineteenth century to the modern era reveals that the bishops, especially including the popes, have drawn the laity to a greater affinity for the scriptures, an affinity that necessarily includes a desire to arrive at a better understanding of what certain passages are intended to convey. This is all in the interest of drawing the faithful closer to ultimate implications of the Bible, whose content stems from divine revelation. As such, this chapter will not so much cover bishops' individual assessments of scriptural excerpts (a fruitfully worthwhile endeavor in and of itself); rather, it will serve as a survey of the elements inherent to the progression of bishops' invitations to the laity to fathom the vast significance of knowing and loving the Word of God.

The Catholic Church and the Origins of the New Testament

The canon of sacred scripture, or what we Christians commonly refer to simply as "the Bible," comprises the forty-six books of the Old Testament and the twenty-seven books of the New Testament. In the first few centuries of church history, Church Fathers such as Saint Athanasius and Saint Jerome solidified the canon of scripture by referring to the forty-six books of the Old Testament that had already been concretized, and doing likewise with the twenty-seven books of the New Testament that had met the three requirements for acceptance into the New Testament canon: apostolic origin, conformity to the rule of faith, and widespread acceptance. This scripture has been handed down by way of divine revelation, and was reinforced by Pope Leo XIII (reigned 1878–1903) in his 1893 encyclical *Providentissimus Deus: On the Study of Holy Scripture*: "This supernatural revelation, according to the belief of the universal Church, is contained both in unwritten Tradition, and in written Books, which are therefore called sacred and canonical. . . ."[1]

In light of the two branches of the deposit of faith, the church, reinforced by the teaching authority referred to as the Magisterium, has always relied on the deposit of faith when it comes to determining how to apply scriptural matters to the sacrament-reinforced faith life of the church, with direct considerations for the laity. In the centuries that followed the era of the Church Fathers, particularly within the breadth of the Middle Ages, the church—with the assistance of devotedly studious monks, prelates, and other lettered figures—endeavored to treat scripture with the

---

1. Leo XIII, *Providentissimus Deus*, 1.

exceeding reverence that it is due. In the modern era, particularly beginning with Pope Leo XIII, the bishops have called the laity to better grasp the Lord's love as exposed through the sacred text.

Pope Leo XIII's Call to Embrace Scripture

Pope Leo XIII was an exemplary force in encouraging a greater understanding of the rudiments of sacred scripture in the wake of the rationalism-imbued ambiance that stemmed from the Enlightenment. The epoch of the mid- to late-1800s was also beset by Modernism, whose tenets were frequently polemical, leading to their treatment by Leo XIII and his successor, Pope Saint Pius X, in particular. Of Leo XIII's myriad writings, *Providentissimus Deus* is a beacon that invites the laity to consider that fathoming sacred scripture is vital to a full life of faith, particularly given that it is the most appreciable grouping of documents regarding the objective narrative of the Paschal Mystery: "Nowhere is there anything more full or more express on the subject of the Savior of the world than is to be found in the whole range of the Bible."[2] Indeed, as we know from within the New Testament, and acutely from within the four canonical Gospels, Jesus relied on the "scriptures" (i.e., the writings sacred to the Jewish people, commonly referred to by Christians as the "Old Testament") during his earthly ministry:

> [Jesus] uses them at times to prove that he is sent by God, and is God himself. From them he cites instructions for his disciples and confirmation of his doctrine. He vindicates them from the calumnies of objectors; he quotes them against Sadducees and Pharisees, and retorts from them upon Satan himself when he dares to tempt him. At the close of his life his utterances are from holy scripture, and it is the holy scripture that he expounds to his disciples after his resurrection, until he ascends to the glory of his Father.[3]

---

2. Ibid., 3.
3. Ibid.

By encouraging proximity to the scriptures in a variety of contexts, always in line with appropriate methodology as facilitated by the Magisterium, Leo XIII's *Providentissimus Deus* has served as a gift to the church in terms of reinvigorating this practice, with the ultimate goal of righteousness that underpins the prospect of eternal life. Aspiring for the sanctity of the faithful, based on the inspiration of the Bible, has been the church's steadfast goal for generation upon generation: "[I]t is owing to the wisdom and exertions of the church that there has been continued from century to century that cultivation of holy scripture which has been so remarkable and has borne such ample fruit."[4] After all, looking to the example of the saints, those holy men and women who have preceded us, Leo XIII reminds us of a key characteristic: "[I]t is well to recall how, from the beginning of Christianity, all who have been renowned for holiness of life and sacred learning have given their deep and constant attention to holy scripture."[5] We would do well to imitate their model.

The faithful, led by the teaching of the bishops, would likewise do well to hope that *Providentissimus Deus* continues to inspire the church to an ever greater acknowledgement of the critical nature of familiarity with the Word of God. Indeed, "Let all, therefore, especially the novices of the ecclesiastical army, understand how deeply the sacred books should be esteemed, and with what greatness and reverence they should approach this great arsenal of heavenly arms."[6] Fortunately, we have the example of loving and guiding prelates who have helped to elucidate the more cumbersome sections: "Judicious theologians and commentators should be consulted as to what is the true or most probable meaning of the passage in discussion. . . ."[7] In the following two sections, you will see how subsequent bishops continued Pope Leo XIII's call, even in the midst of a particularly tumultuous century.

4. Ibid., 6.
5. Ibid., 7.
6. Ibid., 3.
7. Ibid., 23.

THE DEPOSIT OF FAITH

THE TWENTIETH CENTURY AND A RENEWED CALL

In 1920, as the world was still reeling from the aftermath of World War I (1914–1918), Pope Benedict XV (reigned 1914–1922) issued his encyclical *Spiritus Paraclitus: On Saint Jerome*. Benedict XV's intention was for his letter to coincide with the celebrations commemorating the fifteenth centenary of Jerome's death. Saint Jerome's contributions to cementing the structure of the "Bible" per se cannot be overestimated. Jerome's *Vulgate* Bible of AD 382 was the first collection, in one volume, of the sacred scriptures (the forty-six books of the Old Testament and the twenty-seven books of the New Testament), translated into one language: Latin, translated from the original languages of Hebrew and Greek. Continuing in the vein of Pope Leo XIII, in *Spiritus Paraclitus*, Benedict XV endeavors to draw the faithful to all the more appreciate the importance of familiarity with sacred scripture, as transmitted by way of the myriad contributions of that holy man, Saint Jerome. The following assertion rests at the crux of Benedict XV's encyclical: "Would that all Catholics would cling to Saint Jerome's golden rule and obediently listen to their Mother's words, so as modestly to keep within the bounds marked out by the Fathers and ratified by the Church."[8]

Pope Pius XII (reigned 1939–1958) was elected pope just months before the outbreak of World War II on September 1, 1939. On September 30 (the feast of Saint Jerome), 1943, Pius XII issued *Divino Afflante Spiritu: On Promoting Biblical Studies* as a commemoration of the fiftieth anniversary of Leo XIII's *Providentissimus Deus*. It must be stressed that Pius XII's *Divino Afflante Spiritu* was issued in the stark midst of World War II, when the world was in severe need of some semblance of enduring hope, and Pius XII did not shrink from professing his understanding of what was at stake regarding the world's melancholic outlook: "We perceive with greatest sorrow that in not a few has been extinguished the

---

8. Benedict XV, *Spiritus Paraclitus*, 39.

sense not only of Christian moderation and charity, but also of humanity itself."[9]

Returning to the beginning of the text, in his introductory paragraph, Pius XII reminds us of how Leo XIII "safe-guarded the studies of the divine books by most wise precepts and rules."[10] Pius XII goes on to emphasize the importance of undertaking scriptural studies based on accurate methodologies, based on the guidance of holy and orthodox exegetes, and always with utter care. As such, Pius XII fortified Leo XIII's legacy by further encouraging in-depth biblical studies. This is in light of a call for devotedness to the sacred scriptures to an increasing extent on the part of the laity, with all of the faithful joining together to take on "the pious reading and meditation on the sacred scriptures."[11] Pius XII echoes similar sentiments in the penultimate paragraph of his encyclical, in which he offers the following expectation of those experts bestowed with the vocation of biblical exegesis:

> Let the present-day commentators of the sacred scripture emulate, according to their capacity, what those illustrious interpreters of past ages accomplished with such great fruit; so that, as in the past, so also in these days, the Church may have at her disposal learned doctors for the expounding of the divine letters; and, through their assiduous labors, the faithful may comprehend all the splendor, stimulating language, and joy contained in the holy scriptures.[12]

The Bishops, Sacred Scripture, and the Second Vatican Council

It is worthwhile to conclude this overview of the contributions of bishops in modern times regarding sacred scripture and sacred

---

9. Pius XII, *Divino Afflante Spiritu*, [56].
10. Ibid., 1.
11. Ibid., 9.
12. Ibid., 61.

tradition by looking at two documents that were composed in the ambiance of the Second Vatican Council (1962–1965): the Pontifical Biblical Commission's *The Historicity of the Gospels* (1964) and the Vatican II document *Dei Verbum: Dogmatic Constitution on Divine Revelation* (1965). Both of these documents are relatively short, and each can be digested in one sitting.

The Historicity of the Gospels emphasizes the scope of expectations and approaches of the biblical exegete in the modern era in terms of examining the four canonical Gospels, and how the exegete's role is at once challenging and rewarding, given the opportunity to delve more deeply into the Word of God. The five divisions of *The Historicity of the Gospels* are: I) General Guidelines for the Exegete, II) the Elaboration of the Gospel Message, III) Seminary Teachers, IV) Preachers, and V) Biblical Associations.[13] *Dei Verbum* has a similar audience as *The Historicity of the Gospels*, yet it accentuates with greater depth how Divine Revelation remains at the heart of scripture. *Dei Verbum*'s six chapters are: I) Revelation Itself, II) Handing on Divine Revelation, III) Sacred Scripture, Its Inspiration, and Divine Interpretation, IV) the Old Testament, V) the New Testament, and VI) Sacred Scripture in the Life of the Church.[14]

Although this chapter has mentioned various papal documents related to the bishops' call to take ever more seriously the crucial nature of knowing the Bible and holding it to be the Word of God, bishops in other capacities have encouraged the faithful to take up scripture study. This can come in such forms as recommended personal daily reading plans, parish Bible study initiatives, and even formal courses—all the way up to credentialed degree programs—at Catholic colleges and universities. A priority of the bishops continues to be to lead the faithful to better grasp the intention of sacred scripture, as reinforced by the accurate reading of texts as underscored by the Magisterium. It is recommended that the laity gain inspiration from the biblical commentaries and other writings, such those of Pope Benedict XVI (reigned 2005–2013),

---

13. Pontifical Biblical Commission, *The Historicity of the Gospels*, I–V.
14. Paul VI, *Dei Verbum*, I–VI.

who reminds us of the following in his 2010 post-synodal apostolic exhortation *Verbum Domini: On the Word of God in the Life and Mission of the Church*: "I express my hope that the word will be ever more fully at the heart of every ecclesial activity."[15] The benefit is to be steadily enthused by the Psalmist's iconic words: "Your word is a lamp for my feet, a light for my path" (Psalm 119:105).

---

15. Benedict XVI, *Verbum Domini*, 1.

3

Ecology and Environmental Custody
Respecting God's Creation

"Let them know how far more excellent is the Lord than these; for the original source of beauty fashioned them. Or if they were struck by their might and energy, let them from these things realize how much more powerful is he than them. For from the greatness and the beauty of created things their original author, by analogy, is seen."

(Wis 13:3–5)

In the twenty-first century world (and the twenty-first century *world* [read: earth]), few topics result in as many politics-laden discussions as concerns related to the environment in general, one example being how to combat the origins and impact of climate change. Fragile ecosystems are steadily impacted by the degradation of pollution, the annihilation of critically endangered species, a culture of excess and materialism, and other violations of the natural order that ultimately have dire consequences for humanity.

Although the Catholic Church has unfortunately sometimes been regarded as retrograde in its approaches to matters related to the environment and sustainability, anyone so concerned will note that, since the twentieth century, the church has been steadily committed to proclaiming the vast importance of protecting the earth as a feature of God's creation, our tiny abode in the expanse of the universe. Nevertheless, a justifiably recurring theme has been that considerations of the environment as a physical structure, to the unnecessary exclusion of concerns relevant to humanity's status as the pinnacle of God's creation, are in need of reevaluation and reorientation, in the interest of protecting and giving due dignity to human life.

The Bishops' Ongoing Legacy of Respect for Creation

As far as the bishops' dedication to raising concerns regarding how the environment has been threatened by myriad categories of human activity, it is fitting to look at the bishops' writings from the last few decades in particular. This is due in great part to their ability to frame their coverage within the context of the most current scientific research on the causes and effects of threats to God's creation. To say that the bishops have placed this pressing matter within a theological context is to likewise affirm that they have reported on the subsequent necessity of determining and fostering pastoral approaches to resolving the destruction of the environment while underscoring the primacy of humanity within God's plan for creation. This is in the enduring interest of serving the kingdom of God. At the level of the papacy, the last three popes in particular—Saint John Paul II, Benedict XVI, and Francis—have been instrumental leaders by encouraging not only Catholics, but all people of good will, to embrace a restored recognition of the beauty of the natural world as an exhibition of God's boundless goodness and might.

Twenty-five years ago, Saint Pope John Paul II set the far-reaching tone of this watershed historical era by offering the following within the introduction to his message for the January 1,

1990, World Day of Peace, titled "Peace with God the Creator, Peace with All of Creation":

> Faced with the widespread destruction of the environment, people everywhere are coming to understand that we cannot continue to use the goods of the earth as we have in the past. The public in general as well as political leaders are concerned about this problem, and experts from a wide range of disciplines are studying its causes. Moreover, a new *ecological awareness* is beginning to emerge which, rather than being downplayed, ought to be encouraged to develop into concrete programs and initiatives."[1]

In 1991, the year following John Paul II's message for the World Day of Peace 1990, the USCCB issued their pastoral statement *Renewing the Earth: An Invitation to Reflection and Action on Environment in Light of Catholic Social Teaching*. The American bishops continued the conversation that John Paul II ushered in the year prior, prefacing the document by directly referencing the introductory words of the Holy Father's message from the year before. In *Renewing the Earth*, the USCCB covered a variety of points that were in significant need of thorough discussion, especially as they concerned the church's need to provide a theological angle to the critical balance of the natural world. These points included the broader significance of the role of Catholic social teaching vis-à-vis environmental concerns, the call for all Catholics and others of good will to take seriously what is at stake, the appropriate responses necessary, the need for profound reflection upon ecological considerations, the biblical basis for protecting the environment in the interest of the kingdom of God, solidarity with those living in poverty, sustainability and true human development, and other nuanced factors.[2]

---

1. John Paul II, "Peace with God the Creator, Peace with All of Creation," 1.
2. United States Conference of Catholic Bishops, *Renewing the Earth*, I–IV.

The Environment and Distinguishing the Goals of Social Justice

In 2001, ten years after *Renewing the Earth*, the USCCB issued a subsequent pastoral statement related to the environment and social justice, although this one placed a more direct focus on climate change: *Global Climate Change: A Plea for Dialogue, Prudence, and the Common Good*. As its title alludes to, this document places due emphasis on the vital nature of framing this crucial dialogue within the context of the common good of society. At the heart of *Global Climate Change* rests the following challenge by the American bishops when it comes to confronting the damaging effects of man-made climate change:

> Our national debate over solutions to global climate change needs to move beyond the uses and abuses of science, sixty-second ads, and exaggerated claims. Because this issue touches so many people, as well as the planet itself, all parties need to strive for a civil and constructive debate about U.S. decisions and leadership in this area. As people of religious faith, we bishops believe that the atmosphere that supports life on earth is a God-given gift, one we must respect and protect. It unites us as one human family. If we harm the atmosphere, we dishonor our Creator and the gift of creation. The values of our faith call us to humility, sacrifice, and a respect for life and the natural gifts God has provided.[3]

In the same vein as the American bishops, the Canadian bishops have likewise addressed the ethics of caring for the environment, in the interest of the goals of social justice, by issuing their 2003 statement *"You Love All That Exists . . . All Things Are Yours, God, Lover of Life": A Pastoral Letter on the Christian Ecological Imperative from the Social Affairs Commission, Canadian Conference of Catholic Bishops*. The Canadian bishops offered challenges to humanity broadly by emphasizing the elements of social justice that must be included in discussions of the environment and the

---

3. United States Conference of Catholic Bishops, *Global Climate Change*, Conclusion.

wellbeing of humanity, particularly those living on the socio-economic margins: "Ecological problems are enmeshed within social structures that serve the interests of the few at the expense of the many, especially those marginalized and in poverty."[4] The points offered by the American and Canadian bishops at the turn of the twenty-first century have continued well into the modern era, especially in light of the contributions of the two popes at the fore of raising environmental concerns: Benedict XVI and Francis.

Pope Benedict XVI and the Ethics of Sustainability

The pontificate of Pope Benedict XVI was marked by a continued dedication to addressing the concerns that accompany various offenses against the natural world, especially as they constitute menaces to sustainability, causing grave harm to humanity—especially the weakest and most vulnerable—in the process. Even at the outset of his pontificate, during his inaugural homily on April 24, 2005, Benedict offered the following now-iconic advice:

> The external deserts in the world are growing, because the internal deserts have become so vast. Therefore the earth's treasures no longer serve to build God's garden for all to live in, but they have been made to serve the powers of exploitation and destruction. The Church as a whole and all her Pastors, like Christ, must set out to lead people out of the desert, towards the place of life, towards friendship with the Son of God, towards the One who gives us life, and life in abundance.[5]

The reader will note Benedict's allusion to Christ's words in John 10:10, "I came so that they might have life and have it more abundantly." Archbishop Lori of Baltimore makes a similar allusion in *The Joy of Believing*, positing that the *gospel of life* is what "the

---

4. Canadian Conference of Catholic Bishops, *"You Love All That Exists . . . All Things Are Yours, God, Lover of Life,"* 5.

5. Benedict XVI, "Inaugural Pontifical Homily," 4.

church constantly proclaims in fidelity to her Lord, who came to give us abundant life (John 10:10)."[6]

Among other particular initiatives of Benedict's pontificate, there was a marked commitment to highlighting the importance of access to clean water and other comestibles, especially for those mired in material poverty, the reduction of pollutants in the atmosphere, and other specific goals in the interest of sustainability. As one noteworthy example among multiple available, in 2007 the Vatican under Benedict XVI committed to becoming the world's first "carbon-neutral" nation when it announced that it would be converting the Paul VI Auditorium to solar power, as well as planting a forest off-site in Hungary.[7]

The extent of Benedict XVI's pontificate, from 2005 to 2013, featured many similar examples of Benedict's recourse to his Petrine office in order to continually prompt the church to address and defend environmental concerns. Thus, Benedict XVI, the reliably thought-provoking theologian, used his pastoral role to foster a renewed appreciation for the created world as a gift from God. He likewise served as a bridging force between the pontificates of Saint John Paul II and Francis, as the church continued to take ever more seriously the need to protect the environment in the ultimate interests of the kingdom of God.

Pope Francis, the Bishops, and the Priority of Human Life

Pope Francis made history by becoming the first pope to address environmental concerns in the form of an encyclical when he issued his prescient *Laudato Si': On Care for Our Common Home* in May of 2015. *Laudato Si'* has served to capture the attention not only of the Catholic faithful, but of the broader global community as well when it comes to the emphasis that the church has placed on underscoring the need to protect the environment. Of course,

---

6. Lori, *The Joy of Believing*, 171.

7. *Catholic News Agency*, "Vatican Announces Plans to Become First 'Carbon Neutral State' in the World," July 13, 2007.

this comes in the form of steadily looking at the broader situation through a theological lens.

Although various secular sources unfortunately have viewed *Laudato Si'* as more of a political statement than a theological discourse (a more accurate analysis reveals that it features a set of pastoral recommendations that do call for adjustments to policy at various levels of engagement), *Laudato Si'* does not ride along neat ideological tracks; rather, it calls on those of all mindsets and backgrounds to a greater respect for the environment in the interests of serving humanity for the greater glory of the kingdom of God. *Laudato Si'* similarly warrants special consideration in terms of Francis's intended audience, as to which he leaves little wonder: "Now, faced as we are with global environmental deterioration, I wish to address every person living on this planet."[8] Throughout the text, Francis calls on the rhetorical force of his predecessors, making numerous references to John Paul II and Benedict XVI in particular. Francis makes a special effort to highlight the complementary approaches of his pastoral forebears to the ecological crisis in light of ethical polemics by noting the "continuity with the social teaching of the Church"[9] all the way back to the epoch of Saint John XXIII.

Narrowing in on the issue of how some media outlets have unfortunately not noticed the broader implications of *Laudato Si'* as far as the primacy of human life is concerned, it is worthwhile to heed the following direct words from Francis, in which he stresses the need to acknowledge the dignity of the weakest in humanity in the grand scheme of the natural world:

> Since everything is interrelated, concern for the protection of nature is also incompatible with the justification of abortion. How can we genuinely teach the importance of concern for other vulnerable beings, however troublesome or inconvenient they may be, if we fail to protect a

---

8. Francis, *Laudato Si'*, 3.
9. Ibid., 175.

> human embryo, even when its presence is uncomfortable and creates difficulties?[10]

Returning to Francis's efforts to make recourse to the precedents of his predecessors, he follows up this reminder in paragraph 120 by quoting Benedict XVI's 2009 encyclical *Caritatis in Veritate: On Integral Human Development in Charity and Truth*: "If personal and social sensitivity towards the acceptance of a new life is lost, then other forms of acceptance that are valuable for society also wither away,"[11] an allusion to Benedict's own message for the January 1, 2007, World Day of Peace, titled "The Human Person, the Heart of Peace."[12] As we continue into the twenty-first century, the Catholic Church, inspired by the leadership of the bishops, will continue to emphasize the importance of caring for creation. The natural world is a gift from the Lord, intended to be respected and valued, in the interest of our progeny and ultimately of the kingdom of God. God's plan for creation must be honored.

A Brief Mention of the Church's Teachings on Creation and Evolution

To provide a conclusive remark, it is worthwhile to view what the church even means by *creation* per se, because we are not referring to the problematic concept of "creationism." In other words, Catholic doctrine permits an appreciation for the tenets of biological evolution. The twenty-first century world continues to feature the myth that matters of faith are incompatible with matters of physical science, a severe misconception that stems from the Enlightenment. Figures such as Saint John Paul II have combated this mindset, such as in his 1998 encyclical *Fides et Ratio: On the Relationship Between Faith and Reason*. The distinction that the church makes is that, while biological evolution is not inconsistent with broader matters of faith, we must recall that the soul

---

10. Ibid., 120.
11. Benedict XVI, *Caritatis in Veritate*, 28.
12. Benedict XVI, "The Human Person, the Heart of Peace," 5.

originates with God, and is not the result of a biological process, since God had humanity in mind from the beginning of time. John Paul II[13] and Francis[14] in particular have indicated how biological evolution is in keeping with Catholic teaching, with Francis even reminding us of the following as it relates to the Big Bang theory, ushered in by the Belgian Fr. Georges Lemaître, a Catholic priest: "The Big Bang theory, which is proposed today as the origin of the world, does not contradict the intervention of a divine creator but depends on it."[15]

---

13. John Paul II, "Message to the Pontifical Academy of Sciences," 1–7.
14. Francis, "Address to the Pontifical Academy of Sciences," 1–5.
15. Ibid., 3.

4

Ecumenism and Interreligious Dialogue

Striving for God's Will, Striving for Good Will

" . . . so that they may all be one, as you, Father, are in me and I in you, that they also may be in us, that the world may believe that you sent me."

(JOHN 17:21)

There are multiple avenues that the bishops of the world have taken to labor for enduringly positive dynamics, both between Catholics and other Christians (ecumenism) and between Catholics and those of non-Christian faiths (interreligious dialogue). The interest is in dialoguing with those of good will while charitably sharing the truths inherent to the Catholic faith. In a world that is reliably characterized by the tenets of globalization, our Catholic bishops have endeavored to carry out this peace-driven initiative while underscoring and furthering the remarkable treasures of Catholicism, safeguarding the church's dogmas and doctrines that are rooted in the Good News of Jesus Christ.

Ecumenism and Interreligious Dialogue

In order to clear the air, it must be affirmed that there is great worth in fostering substantive ecumenism and interreligious dialogue. Some might question the merits of such an enterprise, but we readily concede that we have made great progress, especially since the twentieth century. Gone are the days—or at least they really should be—in which dialogue between people of different beliefs comes in the form of a cannon blast or the rattling of a sabre. The Catholic Church, led by the example of the bishops, has fostered efforts engendering peace and respect for those of other faiths while delineating what Catholicism contributes to humanity.

Ecumenism, Interreligious Dialogue, and the Second Vatican Council

Ecumenism and interreligious dialogue are not the same as evangelization; however, nor are they the same as proselytism. Evangelization is covered within its own chapter, and of course there are overlaps between dialogue and evangelization; however, proselytism never has any place (although nor is there any place for claims of proselytism where there actually is not any).

In order to more effectively fathom the particular categories of distinction between ecumenism and interreligious dialogue, it is worthwhile to first examine key tenets of the Vatican II document *Unitatis Redintegratio: Decree on Ecumenism*. Note how the following excerpt from chapter 2 (The Practice of Ecumenism) indicates that all of the faithful members of the church—the laity and the clergy (clearly including the bishops) alike—are tasked with the enduring goals of a commitment to fostering good relations between all Christians as brethren in the Lord Jesus Christ:

> The attainment of union is the concern of the whole Church, faithful and shepherds alike. This concern extends to everyone, according to his talent, whether it be exercised in his daily Christian life or in his theological and historical research. This concern itself reveals already to some extent the bond of brotherhood between

all Christians and it helps toward that full and perfect unity which God in his kindness wills.[1]

Just as *Unitatis Redintegratio* was critically formative in terms of fostering unity—if not communion at this juncture in history—between Catholics and other Christians, this excerpt from the conclusion to the document features a call that future generations of bishops within the church have responded to, a call that will be further examined in upcoming sections:

> It is the urgent wish of this Holy Council that the measures undertaken by the sons of the Catholic Church should develop in conjunction with those of our separated brethren so that no obstacle be put in the ways of divine Providence and no preconceived judgments impair the future inspirations of the Holy Spirit.[2]

Whereas *Unitatis Redintegratio* focuses on ecumenism as fruitful dialogue between Christians, a document focusing instead on interreligious dialogue is *Nostra Aetate: Declaration on the Relation of the Church to Non-Christian Religions*. *Nostra Aetate*, although shorter (at approximately half the length of *Unitatis Redintegratio*), has been conceived in a variety of ways as serving as even more of a watershed document from within the pastoral machinations of the Second Vatican Council. In fact, *Nostra Aetate* is such an important document—especially considering the broader reality of our international, intercultural, and pluralistic realm of the twenty-first century—that the faithful should be sure to read this document carefully and purposefully, especially since it is so short than it can be read in one sitting.

Nostra Aetate particularly addresses the church's dialogue with those of the Jewish faith, the Muslim faith, and other mainstream faiths. The document, while short, is substantive insofar as it delineates the fact that, while there are differences between these mainstream faiths, there is also common ground. Due to its call for good will, even when there is theological disagreement, no

1. Paul VI, *Unitatis Redintegratio*, 5.
2. Ibid., 24.

matter how acute, *Nostra Aetate* has set the rhetorical groundwork for many other documents dealing with interreligious dialogue that the bishops have produced since. *Nostra Aetate* opens with these words that have set the tone for its purposes, which existed decades before the globalism-imbued world of the twenty-first century:

> In our time, when day by day mankind is being drawn closer together, and the ties between different peoples are becoming stronger, the Church examines more closely her relationship to non-Christian religions.[3]

In the following sections, you will continue to see the influence of *Unitatis Redintegratio* and *Nostra Aetate*, especially as they concern the employment of fraternal language that should be inherent to the scope of this dialogue, which *Nostra Aetate* alludes to thus: "We cannot truly call on God, the Father of all, if we refuse to treat in a brotherly way any man, created as he is in the image of God."[4] Far beyond the era of the Second Vatican Council, these two documents have served as crucial steps on the path of ecumenism and interreligious dialogue. Before continuing to look at the bishops' contributions to fostering Catholic dialogue with other believers, it is important to understand the value in dialoguing with others of good will at all.

The Goals of Dialogue and Good Will

Returning to ecumenism in particular for a moment, in 1995, thirty years after the close of the Second Vatican Council, well into his pontificate, John Paul II issued his encyclical *Ut Unum Sint: On Commitment to Ecumenism*. John Paul II opens the document by providing a glimpse into the positive ecumenical efforts subsequent to the Council's goals: "The call for Christian unity made by the Second Vatican Ecumenical Council with such impassioned

---

3. Paul VI, *Nostra Aetate*, 1.
4. Ibid., 5.

commitment is finding an ever greater echo in the hearts of believers, especially as the Year 2000 approaches . . ."[5]

Indeed, in the midst of the year 2000, the goals of Pope John Paul II in terms of fostering ecumenism and interreligious dialogue were joined by his fellow bishop, Cardinal Francis Arinze of Nigeria, who served under him as head of the Pontifical Council for Interreligious Dialogue from 1985 to 2002. Within this capacity, Cardinal Arinze undertook substantial efforts at fostering fruitful interreligious dialogue, with unrelenting good will extended to his peers of other faith traditions, while proclaiming the beauty of the Catholic faith with pristine accuracy instead of watering down doctrine, which was a challenging balance to strike if ever there was one. Cardinal Arinze, a prolific writer, has given us two books that cover how to arrive at this pastoral equilibrium: *Meeting Other Believers: The Risks and Rewards of Interreligious Dialogue* (1998) and *Religions for Peace: A Call for Solidarity to the Religions of the World* (2002). The content of these books is comprised of succinct, yet profound, lessons on how to conduct interreligious dialogue while maintaining positive sentiments between those affiliates of varying faith traditions.

In the following two excerpts, note how Cardinal Arinze adeptly achieves the delicate balance of ensuring that interreligious dialogue—which, when undertaken by Catholics, should always be fueled by the charity that underpins the Gospel—is oriented toward all those of good will (rather than becoming tantamount to proselytizing), while simultaneously declaring the need for the faith to be presented accurately:

> The human person has an innate God-given dignity that deserves respect. Religion should be proposed, not imposed. Religious affiliation or unity in belief arrived at as a result of pressure—be that pressure physical, psychological, political, economic, social, or otherwise—is not worthy of the human person. It insults the person on whom it is exerted. It is ignoble of the one who applies

---

5. John Paul II, *Ut Unum Sint*, 1.

> such pressure. It does not do honor to God to whom all true religious acts are directed.[6]

> Interreligious dialogue is a sincere meeting of a person deeply convinced of his own faith, with a believer in another religion. It presupposes peaceful possession of one's religious identity card, and membership in such good standing in one's religious community that one can be named an ambassador of that community.[7]

Elsewhere in *Meeting Other Believers*, Arinze reminds us that, "if we are Catholics, we should not hide this when we meet others. We do not promote dialogue authentically by suppressing our religious identity."[8] Arinze further relies on his characteristic *ambassadorial* language to indicate "how necessary it is for a dialogue partner to have a clear religious image."[9] In this century so replete with pluralistic considerations, Arinze offers the following recommendation in the interest of fostering good will between those of different faiths, while not jeopardizing efforts at spreading the Good News patiently: "Thus it follows that when believers who are culturally and theologically well prepared do listen to one another on matters of belief, many positive advantages can be realized."[10]

The Bishops and Continued Catholic Dialogue with Other Christians

At the turn of the twenty-first century, just as the pontificate of John Paul II featured *Ut Unum Sint*, it was also marked by the development of a document between the Catholic Church and the Lutheran World Federation, the 1999 *Joint Declaration on the Doctrine of Justification*. This served to delineate and clarify nearly 500 years of misunderstandings between Catholics and Lutherans

---

6. Arinze, *Meeting Other Believers*, 67–68.
7. Arinze, *Religions for Peace*, 51.
8. Arinze, *Meeting Other Believers*, 44–45.
9. Ibid., 53.
10. Ibid., 59.

since the beginning of the Protestant Reformation on October 31, 1517. The *Joint Declaration* confesses those areas of shared belief, yet likewise admits those areas in which differences of belief remain. Nevertheless, it was a significant step forward in narrowing the rift between Catholics and Lutherans in particular. As a result of the ecumenical efforts between the two groups, it was possible to declare that, "Our consensus in basic truths of the doctrine of justification must come to influence the life and teachings of our churches."[11] What a fitting outlook, considering that, in 2015, the USCCB's Committee for Ecumenical and Interreligious Affairs joined the Evangelical Lutheran Church in America in publishing their shared document *Declaration on the Way: Church, Ministry, and Eucharist*. This document, rather robust at 120 pages, is of the same ecumenical orientation as the *Joint Declaration*, and in celebrating the multiple steps toward reconciliation, asserts that it "offers encouragement that together Catholics and Lutherans will find ways to move forward where work remains to be done."[12]

Another monumental ecumenical step occurred in February of 2016, when Pope Francis met with Patriarch Kirill, the leader of the Russian Orthodox Church, off-site in Havana, Cuba. This was the first formal encounter ever between the pope and a Russian patriarch, in the nearly 1,000 years since the East-West Schism of 1054. The thirty points that the two men cover within their subsequent *Joint Declaration* provide a sweeping overview of the numerous intersections of doctrine between these two Christian groups, and we are led to ponder the broader significance of their intent as it relates to interreligious dialogue between Christians and non-Christians:

> "In the contemporary world, which is both multiform yet united by a shared destiny, Catholics and Orthodox are called to work together fraternally in proclaiming the Good News of salvation, to testify together to the moral

---

11. Catholic Church and Lutheran World Federation, *Joint Declaration on the Doctrine of Justification*, 43.

12. Unites States Conference of Catholic Bishops and Evangelical Lutheran Church in America, *Declaration on the Way*, 10.

dignity and authentic freedom of the person, 'so that the world may believe' (John 17:21)."[13]

The Bishops and Continued Efforts at Dialogue in the Twenty-First Century

As the twenty-first century advances, the bishops have continued to labor in the interest of encounter in the form of ecumenism and interreligious dialogue. In the wake of unfortunate misunderstandings, such as the misinterpretation (emphasis on *misinterpretation*, as opposed to *inaccuracy*) of Pope Benedict XVI's words offered at the since-deemed "Regensburg Lecture,"[14] the church continues to proclaim the truth in charity when entering into dialogue with those of other faith communities. Documents such as the Pontifical Council for Interreligious Dialogue's 2014 tome *Dialogue in Truth and Charity: Pastoral Orientations for Interreligious Dialogue* have spurred the church to continue laboring for peace while imparting the truth in the midst of a pluralistic world, echoing Cardinal Arinze's prior recommendation regarding cultural and theological competency[15] by positing that, "a sound philosophical and theological formation remains foremost."[16] Other prelates, such as the late Cardinal Francis George, O.M.I., of Chicago, have made special efforts to discuss the specific elements necessary to engage in interreligious dialogue with religious groups, such as with those of the Jewish and Muslim faiths, within two chapters of his 2009 book *The Difference God Makes: A Catholic Vision of Faith, Communion, and Culture*.[17] It is our duty to join them in remaining charitably respectful when presenting the beauty of

---

13. Francis and Kirill, *Joint Declaration of Pope Francis and Patriarch Kirill*, 28.

14. Benedict XVI, "Lecture of the Holy Father," September 12, 2006.

15. Arinze, *Meeting Other Believers*, 59.

16. Pontifical Council for Interreligious Dialogue, *Dialogue in Truth and Charity*, 34.

17. George, *The Difference God Makes*, 77–91, 92–114.

faith. In the midst of attempts at dialogue, the bishops do well to heed this reminder from the Congregation for the Doctrine of the Faith's 2000 declaration *Dominus Iesus: On the Unicity and Salvific Universality of Jesus Christ and the Church*: "In the course of the centuries, the Church has proclaimed and witnessed with fidelity to the Gospel of Jesus."[18]

---

18. Congregation for the Doctrine of the Faith, *Dominus Iesus*, 2.

5

Evangelization
The Good News of Christ is Ever New

"Go, therefore, and make disciples of all nations, baptizing them in the name of the Father, and of the Son, and of the Holy Spirit, teaching them to observe all that I have commanded you. And behold, I am with you always, until the end of the age."
(MATT 28:19–20)

In order to fathom evangelization and how bishops have contributed to this endeavor, it is important to note the goal of *evangelization*: to spread the *Gospel*, the *Good News*, of Jesus Christ. At first glance, such a position may seem simple, if not outright simplistic, but it is critical to focus on a certain aspect of the term: "Good *News*." News implies that which is new; after all, let us remember that "[t]he one who sat on the throne said, 'Behold, I make all things new'" (Rev 21:5).

The bishops of the last few decades since the Second Vatican Council, particularly the last three pontiffs—Saint John Paul II, Benedict XVI, and Francis—have dedicated a great deal of their pastoral attention to how to evangelize, or better said, *re*-evangelize, the world. This has been collectively deemed the "New Evangelization." These last few years, the bishops have devised numerous innovative methods of bringing the Good News not only to non-Christians, but also to the faithful in the pew, who are in need of reinvigoration so that the Gospel may remain ever new to all of Christ's disciples. Evangelization is ultimately an initiative that can be carried out in various ways, based on each disciple's individual gifts. Of course, it is ultimately a work supported by the Holy Spirit, and must always be accompanied by fervent prayer on the part of every faithful disciple, no matter his or her vocation.

Bishops and Highlighting the Need for Ongoing Evangelization

Before entering into a conversation regarding evangelization, no matter the scope of the approach at hand, it is vital to first consider in depth what is at stake: bringing Jesus Christ and the teachings of the Catholic faith to others. Cardinal Wuerl has been a very effective leader at the forefront of the New Evangelization, and his writings on this topic are replete with guiding principles for how to impart the Good News. Thus, Cardinal Wuerl opens his 2010 pastoral letter *Disciples of the Lord: Sharing the Vision—A Pastoral Letter on the New Evangelization* with the following reminder in order to orient our focus: "Christ is the way. When Jesus first came among us, he offered a whole new way of living."[1] Wuerl later offers a similar reminder that we must abide by when undertaking any endeavor related to the New Evangelization: "The first movement of any evangelization originates not in a program, but in a Person, Jesus Christ, the Son of God."[2]

Although there are many joys that come with the New Evangelization, Cardinal Wuerl indicates the dire task that is at hand when it comes to whom we are evangelizing: "[f]or many,

---

1. Wuerl, *Disciples of the Lord*, 3.
2. Ibid., 12.

the invitation has lost its appeal."[3] At the same time, Wuerl does not hesitate to offer examples of the many ways in which we can evangelize on a daily basis:

> The field is rich and the seeds are plenty. Those who have fallen away from the practice of the faith are all around us. We meet them in our workplace. They stand next to us in the grocery line, at the bus stop, and on the Metro. They are in the car next to ours as they wait to pick up their children from sports practice and band rehearsal, and as we go about our daily and weekly errands."[4]

Given that Jesus is at the core of all efforts at evangelization, the enthusiasm that comes with living in loving service to the Lord is what remains at the heart of the impetus of initiatives related to evangelization.

The Bishop's Inculcation of Enthusiasm and Joy in Spreading the Faith

When one has a treasure, such as a love for the Gospel, there is a deep desire to impart that gift. Thus, continuing in *Disciples of the Lord*, Cardinal Wuerl issues the following reminder: "The embrace in the love of Jesus and the joy of his Gospel of new life are meant to be savored, cherished, and shared."[5] Again, we see the same themes of *joy* and *new*ness. Evangelization requires openness on the part of the evangelizer to ongoing evangelization and conversion of him or herself, with the goal of drawing others to Christ by way of the infectious joy that stems only from knowing him.

Indeed, the bishops have fostered and encouraged all Catholics to embrace that same zeal in order to invite others to the Lord, especially those who witness the love with which disciples regard one another and others in their midst: "This is how all will know that you are my disciples, if you have love for one another" (John

---

3. Ibid., 3.
4. Ibid., 15.
5. Wuerl, *Disciples of the Lord*, 6.

3:35); likewise, "your light must shine before others, that they may see your good deeds and glorify your heavenly Father" (Matt 5:16). This attitude of evangelization rooted in discipleship and love for the Lord, accompanied by the need for ongoing conversion in consideration of the newness of the Gospel, is alluded to in a segment of Saint Pope John Paul II's 1999 apostolic exhortation *Ecclesia in America: On the Encounter with the Living Jesus Christ—The Way to Conversion, Communion, and Solidarity in America*:

> Conversion, therefore, fosters a new life, in which there is no separation between faith and works in our daily response to the universal call to holiness. In order to speak of conversion, the gap between faith and life must be bridged. Where this gap exists, Christians are such only in name. To be true disciples of the Lord, believers must bear witness to their faith . . ."[6]

It is perhaps little coincidence that, just the year prior to publishing *Ecclesia in America*, John Paul II's 1998 *ad limina* addresses to the bishops of the United States became collectively referred to as the *springtime of evangelization*. Thus, the following was offered by the Holy Father in a letter to Cardinals Hickey (of Washington) and Keeler (of Baltimore) of March 17, 1998: "Evangelization is the Church's effort to proclaim to everyone that God loves them, that he has given himself for them in Christ Jesus, and that he invites them to an unending life of happiness. Once this Gospel has been accepted as the 'good news,' it demands to be shared."[7] Yet again, the prospect of love and joy erupt into the equation, with the bishops taking up this work of the New Evangelization in order to offer hope to those open to the Good News, current and potential Catholics alike.

---

6. John Paul II, *Ecclesia in America*, 26.
7. Williams, *Springtime of Evangelization*, 55.

The New Evangelization, Benedict XVI and Francis, and Culture

Benedict and Francis continued the labors of the New Evangelization that John Paul II had furthered so well. In 2005, Benedict used the occasion of his first encyclical, *Deus Caritas Est: On Christian Love*, to reinforce the understanding that efforts at evangelization should feature an especially charitable scope, indicating that, "it is often possible to establish a fruitful link between evangelization and works of charity."[8] Benedict also provides the connotation of action inherent to spreading the Gospel with the following excerpt from his 2007 encyclical *Spe Salvi: On Christian Hope*:

> Christianity was not only "good news"—the communication of a hitherto unknown content. In our language we would say: the Christian message was not only "informative" but "performative." That means: the Gospel is not merely a communication of things that can be known—it is one that makes things happen and is life-changing."[9]

Living the Gospel with joy is a mindset of evangelization not only for the individual, in terms of allowing oneself to be ever open to the Good News; rather, it is likewise an approach when it comes to spreading the Good News to the multitude, which can hardly be done with gloom or negativity, let alone manifestations of uncertainty. The joy that is necessary is a factor underpinning efforts at evangelization that have continued from the pontificate of Benedict XVI to Francis. Just as Benedict emphasizes aspects of joy within his encyclicals *Deus Caritas Est* of 2005 and *Spe Salvi* of 2007, Francis maintains this outlook in two key documents issued in 2013, the first year of his pontificate: his encyclical *Lumen Fidei: On Faith* and his apostolic exhortation *Evangelii Gaudium: On the Proclamation of the Gospel in Today's World*.

The opening lines of *Evangelii Gaudium* resonate with the newness of the Gospel, with the joy that comes with imparting the Good News to others, always undergirded by enduring love:

---

8. Benedict XVI, *Deus Caritas Est*, 30.
9. Benedict XVI, *Spe Salvi*, 2.

The joy of the Gospel fills the hearts and lives of all who encounter Jesus. Those who accept his offer of salvation are set free from sin, sorrow, inner emptiness, and loneliness. With Christ joy is constantly born anew.[10]

Pope Francis, as the first pope from Latin America (and of all the Americas at that), has placed great emphasis on fostering a *culture of encounter*, and this is a critical aspect of sharing the Good News. Indeed, Pope Francis's encouragement of encountering others is complementary to his Jesuit charism of accommodation, indeed, recognizing the particular characteristics and attributes of others—both as individuals and as cultures—in order to align the Christian message to meet them where they are, and similarly emphasizing that, "it is imperative to evangelize cultures in order to inculturate the Gospel."[11]

Two other bishops of note, Cardinal Wuerl and the late Cardinal George, whose roles as prelates bridged the pontificates of both Benedict XVI and Francis, have remarked on the need to recognize the irreplaceable importance of cultural considerations when undertaking the New Evangelization. For example, Wuerl has noted that "culture is the field of the New Evangelization. Culture refers to the daily ethos, the various networks of understanding and meaning that give rise to the many everyday connections between the person, community, and society."[12] Similarly, Cardinal George underscored that, "to form Gospel-shaped people, the Church must work to create Gospel-friendly cultures."[13] In the midst of these discussions of the merits of a cultural scope when it comes to evangelizing, continuing into the twenty-first century, Pope Francis and the bishops have likewise indicated that there are various challenges inherent to imparting the Good News.

---

10. Francis, *Evangelii Gaudium*, 1.
11. Ibid., 69.
12. Wuerl, *Disciples of the Lord*, 21.
13. George, *The Difference God Makes*, 26.

Overcoming Impediments to Evangelization with Innovation and Zeal

There are various impediments to the New Evangelization, and they come in such forms as materialism, consumerism, selfishness, and other elements that take away from the openness to the Gospel that is inherent to the human heart. Around the globe, there are also more objectively palpable factors, such as geographical inaccessibility, illiteracy, and governmental structures that are hostile to missionaries—whether official or *de facto*—laboring to bring the Word of God into their lands. The bishops have led the church to seek ways to overcome these obstacles.

In his 2013 book *New Evangelization: Passing on the Catholic Faith Today*, Cardinal Wuerl reminds us thus: "Today, the New Evangelization must show a *boldness* born of confidence in Christ."[14] Cardinal Wuerl has likewise reminded us of the particular patience that must be in place: "The growth of the seed takes time."[15] Despite the challenges that are presented in the midst of the New Evangelization, the laity remains grateful for courageous and considerate bishops whose interest is in shepherding souls toward the Good Shepherd (cf. John 10:1–21). Cardinal Wuerl further places the matter in perspective by laying the task before us while further alluding to this analogy of planting seeds:

> Planting the seed may mean that we learn new styles of communication, open our hearts to a more culturally diverse community, study more deeply the mysteries of the faith, reach out with confidence and invite a neighbor to attend Mass, forgive a long-held grudge, or focus on a new and more influential approach with a son or daughter, father or mother, or spouse who is away from the practice of the faith.[16]

Regarding these *new styles of communication*, it is incumbent upon our bishops to become familiar with the means of broadcast

---

14. Wuerl, *New Evangelization*, 86.
15. Wuerl, *Disciples of the Lord*, 21.
16. Ibid., 23.

communication—especially considering electronic mass media—that permit their message to be spread far and wide, in ways unimaginable 500 years ago, or even when the New Evangelization began just decades ago. Bishops would do well to "put out into deep water" (see Luke 5:4) by using popular social media platforms, podcasts, and so forth, in order to draw more souls to know the Good News of Jesus Christ. Bishops can also post homilies and pastoral letters online, and in this age of great literacy, many lay Catholics eagerly await new books, essays, and other writings from their bishops (hence, a significant aim of this book). Bishops such as Robert Barron, auxiliary bishop of the Archdiocese of Los Angeles, Cardinal Luis Antonio Tagle of Manila, and Cardinal Wuerl readily use the internet to advance the Good News far and wide.

In order to provide encouragement when it comes to taking on this innovative approach to evangelization in the midst of the Digital Age, it is worthwhile to conclude with Pope Benedict XVI's words that he shared with the diplomatic corps on January 9, 2006, months into his pontificate, which was already marked by a particular zeal for evangelization. Note Benedict's allusion to Saint Paul, a model for evangelization as the "Apostle to the Gentiles": "The Church's task is none other than to spread the message of Christ, who came, as Saint Paul writes in the Letter to the Ephesians, to proclaim peace to those far away and to those who are near" (cf. Eph 2:17).[17] May such an outlook remain at the core of the church's efforts at evangelization, led by faithful pastors endeavoring to expand and nurture the Lord's flock.

---

17. Benedict XVI, *Saint Paul: Spiritual Thoughts Series*, 78.

6

Human Sexuality
Treasuring God's Remarkable Plan

"Do you not know that your body is a temple of the Holy Spirit within you, whom you have from God, and that you are not your own? For you have been purchased at a great price. Therefore, glorify God in your body."

(1 COR 6:19–20)

Human sexuality is a topic that has justifiably earned much attention from the bishops over the course of the last fifty years. As sexual norms that were once taken for granted are disregarded, and as formerly standardized conceptualizations of sexual conventions are loosened around the globe, especially in the West, the bishops have had to steadily remind the laity of our common call to chastity. The popes and bishops, while sometimes in disagreement regarding where priorities reside, have for the most part been concerted in their efforts to proclaim the beautiful gift of human sexuality, properly understood and properly expressed.

Various challenges remain on this front, as bishops have had to grapple with menaces to a more chaste comprehension of human sexuality. This is particularly relevant in circumstances in which the church has spoken in opposition to lifestyles that are at odds with Christ's teachings. In these scenarios, the activity itself is the area of concern, rather than the person himself or herself. Continuing in the twenty-first century, the bishops will have to emphasize that the church's teachings about human sexuality—although hardly popular in modern times—ultimately reflect the hope that living chastely will aid societies around the globe to be more open to considering the inherent human dignity and worth that each of us celebrates.

The Bishops' Emphasis on the Complementary Nature of Man and Woman

A worthwhile point of departure for discussing how the bishops have addressed human sexuality is the manner in which they have indicated the complementary nature of man and woman in God's plan for humanity. This has been one of Pope Francis's prime goals since his pontificate began in 2013. For example, in his first papal document, the 2013 encyclical *Lumden Fidei*, Francis shares elements of the theological understanding of the nature of man and woman united as husband and wife, and how the family, united in love, features expressions marked by sexual differentiation:

> The first setting in which faith enlightens the human city is the family. I think first and foremost of the stable union of man and woman in marriage. This union is born of their love, as a sign and presence of God's own love, and of the acknowledgment and acceptance of the goodness of sexual differentiation, whereby spouses can become one flesh (cf. Gen 2:24) and are enabled to give birth to a new life, a manifestation of the Creator's goodness, wisdom, and loving plan.[1]

Continuing this focus, in November 2014, the Vatican hosted a colloquium titled "The Complementarity of Man and Woman

---

1. Francis, *Lumen Fidei*, 52.

in Marriage." Pope Francis provided remarks for the occasion, in which he indicated the unfortunate confusion that has arisen in modern times regarding the gifts that both men and women bring to their marriages, always in the interest of their children as a united family. Note Pope Francis's continued encouragement of society to offer greater recognition of both the distinctness and equality of men and women in the midst of celebrating the marital covenant when he states that, "complementarity will take many forms as each man and woman brings his or her distinctive contributions to their marriage and to the formation of their children."[2]

Thus, on various other occasions within the last few decades, the bishops have spoken and written about the multitudinous gifts that men and women have contributed to humanity within their respective roles. A noteworthy document from Saint John Paul II is his 1988 apostolic letter *Mulieris Dignitatem: On the Dignity and Vocation of Women on the Occasion of the Marian Year*. John Paul II reminded us:

> From the beginning of Christ's mission, women show to him and to his mystery a special sensitivity which is characteristic of their femininity. It must also be said that this is especially confirmed in the Paschal Mystery, not only at the Cross but also at the dawn of the Resurrection.[3]

Bishops have likewise called on men to value their particular role, as Bishop Thomas Olmsted of Phoenix achieves in his 2015 *Into the Breach: An Apostolic Exhortation to Catholic Men*. In this letter, Bishop Olmsted reminds us what is expected of men, given the need to serve as a protector and defender:

> Herein lies the fullness of masculinity; each Catholic man must be prepared to give himself completely, to charge into the breach, to engage in spiritual combat, to defend women, children, and others against the wickedness and snares of the devil![4]

2. Vatican Radio, "Pope Francis: Marriage and the Family Are in Crisis," November 11, 2014.
3. John Paul II, *Mulieris Dignitatem*, 16.
4. Olmsted, *Into the Breach*, 10.

Various other bishops have underscored the value in acknowledging the complementary nature of men and women. This is especially vital as the faithful require guidance in terms of discerning their vocation. At the same time, the bishops have done well to emphasize the inherent equality between the sexes. After all, as Saint John Paul II has affirmed, "both man and woman are human beings to an equal degree, both are created in God's image."[5]

Matters of Human Sexuality Following the Second Vatican Council

After the Second Vatican Council, there was a successive wave of bishops, with the Vatican at the fore of course, dedicated to indicating to the laity the vast beauty of God's plan for human sexuality. These documents have been met with mixed responses from the laity, and there is unfortunately widespread dissent on the part of many Catholics who decline to see the enduring merit in honoring the church's teachings on human sexuality. However, each of these documents should be seen as they are intended: to reflect Christ's own teachings as they relate to avoiding acts of "unchastity" (see Matt 15:19; cf. Mark 7:21 and Rev 9:21).

A watershed document of the post-Vatican II era was Blessed Pope Paul VI's 1968 encyclical *Humanae Vitae: On the Regulation of Birth*, most famous for solidifying the church's teachings against the use of artificial birth control. As we see during the modern era rife with sexual promiscuity, what *Humanae Vitae* portended has summarily come true, and the world yearns for the benefits of a greater embrace of chastity. The laity would do well to read *Humanae Vitae* in its entirety, particularly given its succinctness yet fullness of pastoral dynamism, bearing in mind the particular "need to create an atmosphere favorable to the growth of chastity so that true liberty may prevail over license...."[6]

---

5. John Paul II, *Mulieris Dignitatem*, 6.
6. Paul VI, *Humanae Vitae*, 21.

In the decades following the Second Vatican Council, as the Sexual Revolution raged through the West, wreaking havoc on families and shaking the very foundations of the institution of marriage, the bishops remained resolute in their defense of the church's teachings on matters of human sexuality. Many individual episcopal conferences provided directives that covered their respective geographic areas and nations. For example, the USCCB (then United States Catholic Conference) reminded us in their 1990 document *Human Sexuality: A Catholic Perspective for Education and Lifelong Learning*: "Each of us is entrusted by God with the responsibility to guide and direct this gift wisely and lovingly. At best, our sexuality calls us to personal maturity and interpersonal commitments."[7] Documents that the Vatican produced during this epoch include the Congregation for the Doctrine of the Faith's 1975 *Persona Humana: Declaration on Certain Questions Concerning Sexual Ethics* (still during the pontificate of Paul VI), the Congregation for Catholic Education's 1983 *Educational Guidance in Human Love: Outlines for Sex Education* (during the pontificate of John Paul II), and the Pontifical Council for the Family's 1995 *The Truth and Meaning of Human Sexuality: Guidelines for Education within the Family* (also during the pontificate of John Paul II).

A document that deserves special mention is the Congregation for the Doctrine of the Faith's 1986 *Letter to the Bishops of the Catholic Church on the Pastoral Care of Homosexual Persons*. This document emphasizes that the Catholic Church's teaching on sexuality activity as only permissible between a husband and wife in marriage does not mean that those of any category of sexual orientation are somehow excluded from participation in the church. Likewise, the church insists that there is never any setting within which someone's intrinsic human dignity should be jeopardized, as emphasized by then-Cardinal Ratzinger:

> It is deplorable that homosexual persons have been and are the object of violent malice in speech or in action. Such treatment deserves condemnation from the

---

7. United States Conference of Catholic Bishops, *Human Sexuality*, 10.

Church's pastors wherever it occurs. It reveals a kind of disregard for others which endangers the most fundamental principles of a healthy society. The intrinsic dignity of each person must always be respected in word, in action, and in law.[8]

Since the pontificate of Saint John Paul II, the church's bishops have continued to issue documents and statements in the interest of not simply adopting a defensive position or putting up walls against the world as a flood of governmental legislation and cultural exercises strive to normalize that which is controversial within the realm of human sexuality; rather, bishops have begun to take on the task of emphasizing the positive elements inherent to the church's time-tested teachings on the merits of chaste living according to God's plan for human sexuality.

Pope Francis and Opposition to "Ideological Colonization"

A matter that the bishops have addressed in recent years is the advance of so-designated "gender theory" and "ideological colonization." Pope Francis has been at the forefront of this opposition, and has repeatedly spoken out against this trend. Some examples include on his return flight from the Philippines in January 2015, when he confronted ideological colonization, especially in matters concerning the promise of financial assistance by Western nations being tied to the imposition of controversial standards of sexual morality.[9] Pope Francis addressed this matter yet again in August 2015, when addressing bishops of the Caribbean, as reported by Vatican Radio: "Stressing the need to focus on the pastoral care of the family, Pope Francis also spoke of the challenge of gender

---

8. Congregation for the Doctrine of the Faith, *Letter to the Bishops of the Catholic Church on the Pastoral Care of Homosexual Persons*, 10.

9. *National Catholic Register*, "Pope Francis Warns West Over 'Ideological Colonization,'" January 20, 2015.

ideology in his prepared remarks which were handed to the bishops during the audience."[10]

Pope Francis's rejection of ideological colonization continued during his apostolic visit to the United States in September 2015, which included his presence at the World Meeting of Families in Philadelphia. Speaking to the United Nations in New York City on September 25, Francis commented on the dilemma of "carrying out an ideological colonization by the imposition of anomalous models and lifestyles which are alien to people's identity and, in the end, irresponsible."[11] Nearly a year later, on July 27, 2016, Francis focused on the challenges that gender ideology poses to children in particular in his address to the bishops of Poland:

> Today children—children!—are taught in school that everyone can choose his or her sex. Why are they teaching this? Because the books are provided by the persons and institutions that give you money. These forms of ideological colonization are also supported by influential countries.[12]

The Bishops, the Laity, and Chastity in the Twenty-First Century

There are various other challenges that the bishops have faced regarding how to proclaim the church's teachings on human sexuality and the inherent dignity of the person. One such obstacle is the scourge of pornography that has led to the degradation of the human person and to the destruction of so many relationships. Individual bishops and bishops' conferences have addressed this dilemma in recent years. In 2014, Bishop Paul Loverde of Arlington,

---

10. Vatican Radio, "Marriage Between Man and Woman, No to Gender Ideology," June 8, 2015.

11. Francis, "Address of the Holy Father—Meeting with the Members of the General Assembly of the United Nations Organization," September 25, 2015, 16.

12. Francis, "Dialogue of the Holy Father with the Bishops of Poland," July 27, 2016.

Virginia, issued his pastoral letter *Bought with a Price: Every Man's Duty to Protect Himself and His Family from a Pornographic Culture*, thus setting before us why pornography is so pernicious: "It obscures and destroys people's ability to see one another as unique and beautiful expressions of God's creation, instead darkening their vision, causing them to view others as objects to be used and manipulated."[13] In the following year, the USCCB issued their statement on pornography *Create in Me a Clean Heart: A Pastoral Response to Pornography*, whose title is based on Psalm 51:12: "A clean heart create for me, God; renew within me a steadfast spirit." *Create in Me a Clean Heart* emphasizes the importance of understanding the broader scope of chastity by explaining that, "chastity integrates our internal desires for sexual pleasure into our overall pursuit of moral excellence and holiness."[14]

In 2016, Pope Francis gave us his post-synodal apostolic exhortation, *Amoris Laetitia: On Love in the Family*. Among other considerations, Francis has underscored the importance of chastity in light of preparation for marital union, despite the multiple challenges to a fitting understanding of human sexuality, properly understood, in modern times:

> The complexity of today's society and the challenges faced by the family require a greater effort on the part of the whole Christian community in preparing those who are about to be married. The importance of the virtues needs to be included. Among these, chastity proves invaluable for the genuine growth of love between persons.[15]

Even in the midst of twenty-first century challenges, the bishops will hopefully continue to encourage chastity. They can likewise remind the laity that it is indeed humanly possible to embrace chastity in the interest of purity, recalling the words of 2 Tim 1:7: "For God did not give us a spirit of cowardice but rather of power and love and self-control." It is worthwhile to close with the

---

13. Loverde, *Bought with a Price*, 15.

14. United States Conference of Catholic Bishops, *Create in Me a Clean Heart*, 3.

15. Francis, *Amoris Laetitia*, 206.

prudent words of Blessed Paul VI from his prophetic encyclical *Humanae Vitae*: "But to those who consider this matter diligently, it will indeed be evident that this endurance enhances man's dignity and confers benefits on human society."[16]

---

16. Paul VI, *Humanae Vitae*, 20.

7

Immigrants and Refugees
Recognizing Our Brethren

"So then you are no longer strangers and sojourners, but you are fellow citizens with the holy ones and members of the household of God . . . "

(Eph 2:19)

It is opportune to open this chapter with a brief, yet cogent, passage from Deuteronomy: "So you too should also love the resident alien, for that is what you were in the land of Egypt" (10:19). The topic of immigration, immigration reform, and refugees compels the faithful to tap into a profound consideration of God's mercy. It is unfortunately typical to be "put off" by those who are of a different country of origin, nationality, language, and/or culture. However, the demands of the Gospel are to care for those in our midst, and to view them not as "the other," but as fellow denizens of this life, and hopefully of the next as well.

Over the course of the last few decades, bishops around the world have been dedicated to underscoring the church's teachings on the importance of caring for the immigrant, because it is in doing so that we witness the face of Christ in the form of a stranger and welcome him or her (see Matt 25:35). Of particular concern has been the international refugee crisis, especially regarding those who have fled from various enclaves within the Middle East for the sake of not only their livelihoods, but of their very lives themselves. In the midst of this ongoing refugee crisis, it is important for the faithful to recall, based on the bishops' promptings, the crucial nature of extending charity and welcome to the migrant and the refugee.

Recalling That We Are All Immigrants

We are all immigrants. No matter our current geographic location, national affiliation, citizenship, or other designation, we are all immigrants, be it one generation or multiple generations ago. There are too many myths circulating regarding who comprises immigrants and who does not. In the interest of social justice, bishops of various countries have spoken and written about the importance of viewing immigration as a human rights issue; in other words, it is a reality whose ethical underpinnings are found in the sacred scriptures, and it is therefore ultimately oriented toward the kingdom of God. As Bishop Nicholas DiMarzio of Brooklyn, who has also served as the executive director of the USCCB's Migration and Refugee Services and as a member of the Pontifical Council for the Pastoral Care of Migrants and Itinerant People, has invited us to recall via his 2008 book *Brothers and Sisters in Christ: A Catholic Teaching on the Issue of Immigration*:

> Immigration has been called a theologizing experience in the sense that uprooting often leads people to a recognition of their true and genuine roots in God. From biblical times to now, migration has always been one of the ways that we as a people have encountered God.[1]

Looking at the United States—a nation of immigrants if ever there was one—specifically for a moment draws us to fathom that immigration has been a prominent feature of the history of this

---

1. DiMarzio, *Brothers and Sisters in Christ*, 37.

grandiose nation. Regarding immigration to the United States from majority Catholic countries, such as Ireland, Italy, Poland, and others, there was a great deal of discrimination heaped upon them during the 1800s and early 1900s in particular. As such, the bishops of the United States have endeavored to remind both their flocks and everyone of good will that the Catholic Church is committed to promoting and ensuring that this nation continues to permit immigrants to substantively offer the gift of their presence in order to enrich and strengthen our remarkable national tapestry.

The Bishops and Immigration Reform

The bishops reliably reinforce that reasonable immigration reform is warranted in order to facilitate standards whereby migrants are capable of making their way around in order to foster a better life for themselves and their families. The bishops and others of good will do not foster legislative rigidity or intolerance when it comes to the circumstances of migrants and refugees; yet, nor do they condone lawlessness and chaos. To reiterate, attempts at *reasonable* immigration reform are understandable. As Bishop DiMarzio has offered, "there are times when Catholics are asked to work for the change of laws, while at the same time obeying laws where the rights of conscience are not violated."[2] Subsequently, speaking about the situation of the United States in particular:

> Most immigrants, however, are not criminals in any standard sense of the term. Most simply want to work hard, provide for their families, and practice their faith. We must go beyond the issue of law here to find out what motivates immigrants to come to our country.[3]

Looking at the situation beyond the United States, the USCCB has placed the matter of immigration reform in an international context by raising concerns about how to best accommodate

2. Ibid., 8.
3. Ibid., 9.

refugees while respecting the rule of law. As with any other ethical consideration, it is necessary to look at the root of the issue at hand. Note the following recommendation offered by the USCCB in their 2000 statement *Welcoming the Stranger Among Us: Unity in Diversity*, a document particularly relevant in light of the refugee crises at this point in the twenty-first century:

> The ultimate resolution of the problems associated with forced migration and illegal immigration lies in changing the conditions that drive persons from their countries of origin. Accordingly, we urge the governments of the world, particularly our own government, to promote a just peace in those countries that are at war, to protect human rights in those countries that deny them, and to foster the economic development of those countries that are unable to provide for their own peoples. We also urge the governments of the "receiving" countries to welcome these immigrants, to provide for their immediate needs, and to enable them to come to self-sufficiency as quickly as possible.[4]

An aim of the bishops has been to bring the voice of the church into the public square when it comes to how to best address immigration reform. Since migration has been a human reality for as long as there has been humanity, it is necessary to view the immigrant or the refugee as a human being first and foremost. In order to further place the matter in the lens of that which warrants reasonable reform while still respecting the needs of the individual and the family, Archbishop José Gómez of the Archdiocese of Los Angeles reminds us of the need to frame political discourse according to the moral implications of immigration policy. In his 2013 book *Immigration and the Next America: Renewing the Soul of Our Nation*, Gómez observes: "Our political speech these days expresses the disorder of our public moral reasoning, as we try to justify what can't be justified."[5] As such, our bishops will continue

---

4. United States Conference of Catholic Bishops, *Welcoming the Stranger Among Us*.

5. Gómez, *Immigration and the Next America*, 10.

to embrace immigration reform that coincides with fundamental standards of ethics and morality in the interest of social justice, reflective of the Gospel.

The Contributions of Immigrants to the Kingdom of God

To examine immigration with a theological perspective draws us to a greater appreciation of the myriad gifts that immigrants have brought to their communities. It must be posited that since human beings are never an object, and thus cannot be objectified or seen as a means by any measure of the imagination, it would be inaccurate to pretend that an immigrant is only as important as whatever he or she can demonstrably deliver to others. Nor would it be correct to view someone as an immigrant solely as if being so were that person's primary social categorization. To do so would be tantamount to a skewed comprehension of our inherent human dignity, which is always independent of our particularly perceived functions within society, whether locally, regionally, nationally, or internationally. Returning to the reality that we are all immigrants, it is still incumbent upon us to fathom that fellow sojourners, be they migrant workers, refugees from political turmoil, or anyone in any other situation, are foremost our brethren who participate in society just like anyone else, as we work out our journey with the Lord simultaneously.

In the same vein that we celebrate other people's gifts that they bring to any community setting, it is equally important for us to highlight the numerous contributions that immigrants have offered, in order to underscore that they are participants in society just like those living in a more stable lifestyle. In fact, we should greatly appreciate the contributions made by those who have already had to overcome seemingly insurmountable odds. Note how Cardinal George emphasized the considerable status of migrants in the twenty-first century in his 2011 book *God in Action: How Faith in God Can Address the Challenges of the World*:

The Church holds that the migrant is first of all a gift and not a problem. The Church has voiced this conviction, which derives from God's activity as creator, in different ways and in various forums during the last decades, in which we have experienced the increasing pace of migration flows everywhere on the planet.[6]

Bishop DiMarzio offers a similar assessment, this time reinforcing how immigrants contribute not merely by sociological metrics, but exceedingly more considerably, in terms of how they enrich and diversify the church:

> Immigrants bring many benefits to our country. They become the new life's blood of those citizens striving to better their human condition. In doing so, they bring new energy and new diversity to a land built by immigrants. They also help our economy by working in important industries. They also can teach us much on spirituality and the worship of God.[7]

Although Bishop DiMarzio's assessment is primarily oriented toward immigrants in the United States, his outlook is reflective of the contributions of immigrants worldwide. It should be every Catholic's hope that the bishops continue to underscore the contributions of immigrants of any classification. In doing so, the church will continue to embrace its mission of building up the kingdom of God through the participation of all of our brethren, of any background or circumstance.

The Work of Bishops to Continue Welcoming Immigrants and Refugees

As the twenty-first century advances, the bishops shall continue to uphold the rights and dignity of immigrants, in order to allow them to partake in the offerings of broader society, therefore allowing them access to ways to contribute to the kingdom of God

---

6. George, *God in Action*, 165.
7. DiMarzio, *Brothers and Sisters in Christ*, 36.

during their time as fellow sojourners here in the world. Examples abound of bishops calling on the global community—especially world leaders—to take seriously the plight of migrants and refugees as they attempt to forge a settled and more peaceful existence for themselves and their families. Pope Francis has led the way, both through his word and personal example, including by collaborating with other religious leaders. For instance, he has met with Orthodox leaders to accommodate migrants in the midst of the Syrian refugee crisis that has racked the world as of the mid-2010s.[8]

Episcopal conferences have likewise joined forces to speak up for the needs of migrants around the globe. As a case in point, in 2003, the United States Conference of Catholic Bishops joined the Conferencia del Episcopado Mexicano ("Mexican Bishops' Conference") in issuing the joint statement *Strangers No Longer: Together on the Journey of Hope*, which indicated the need for the international community, including various episcopal conferences, to labor together in the interest of proclaiming the human rights and inherent dignity of migrants around the globe, underscoring that violations of these rights must be opposed since they ultimately offend God's plan for humanity:

> We speak as two episcopal conferences but as one Church, united in the view that migration between our two nations is necessary and beneficial. At the same time, some aspects of the migrant experience are far from the vision of the kingdom of God that Jesus proclaimed: many persons who seek to migrate are suffering, and, in some cases, tragically dying; human rights are abused; families are kept apart; and racist and xenophobic attitudes remain."[9]

Just as the American Catholic bishops have done, in documents such as their 2000 statement *Welcoming the Stranger Among*

---

8. Catholic Herald, "Pope Francis and Orthodox Leaders Call on International Community to Respond to Refugee Crisis," April 18, 2016.

9. United States Conference of Catholic Bishops and the Mexican Bishops' Conference, *Strangers No Longer*, 2.

Us,[10] the Canadian bishops have emphasized the need to look at the root causes of immigration. One such example is the Canadian Conference of Catholic Bishops' 2006 *We Are Aliens and Transients Before the Lord Our God: A Pastoral Letter on Immigration and the Protection of Refugees*: "Unless the root causes of migration are addressed in terms of violence, ecological degradation, and social inequality, more and more people will be forced to move."[11]

A point of reflection is due, from the bishops of Arizona's 2005 document *You Welcomed Me: A Pastoral Letter on Migration Released on the Feast of Our Lady of Guadalupe* (December 12): "Let us strive to open our hearts to the newcomers in our midst, find ways to celebrate the growing cultural and ethnic diversity of our parishes, and invite immigrant families into active parish life."[12] Such a perspective, rooted in the Gospel, ultimately reflects the attitude to which all Catholics are called, given that either we or our ancestors were immigrants at one point or another. The bishops' emphasis on the charity that is due to every migrant provides hope for a peaceful world, to the greater glory of the kingdom of God.

---

10. United States Conference of Catholic Bishops, *Welcoming the Stranger Among Us.*

11. Canadian Conference of Catholic Bishops, *We Are Aliens and Transients Before the Lord Our God*, 20.

12. Arizona Catholic Conference, *You Welcomed Me*, 4.

8

International Relations
Healing a Broken World

" . . . for you are all one in Christ Jesus."
(GAL 3:28B)

This chapter may at first glance seem superfluous, since there are already other chapters dealing with how the bishops have addressed such considerations as immigration, ecumenism and interreligious dialogue, evangelization throughout the international realm, peace and opposition to war and terrorism, and the persecution of the church around the globe, among other similar situations. However, it is worthwhile to take the time to appreciate the myriad ways in which the bishops have led the faithful by proclaiming the Good News on an international scale. This ecclesial activity has included dialoguing with other bishops around the world and relying on their pastoral roles to see how their support of their fellow bishops can aid in fostering unity in the church as a whole.

Given that the twenty-first century is replete with globalization, bishops do well to be increasingly savvy when it comes to framing the Gospel in terms that most effectively permit the Good

News to be imparted far and wide around the world. Fortunately, the Digital Age—which admittedly features some drawbacks (in fact, more than can be adequately covered here)—provides for the rapid transmission of dispatches that facilitate cohesion in terms of ensuring that unity and fraternity are goals of intra-ecclesial dialogue. Indeed, compared to previous eras of not that long ago (even decades ago, really), when thousands of miles separated prominent figureheads around the globe, it is crucial for the faithful in modern times to take advantage of technological innovations when it comes to participating in the privilege of sharing the Good News on a global scale.

A feature of this chapter is that it is centered significantly on four papal documents—the Vatican II document *Ad Gentes: Decree on the Mission Activity of the Church* (1965), and three of Pope Saint John Paul II's post-synodal apostolic exhortations, *Ecclesia in Africa: On the Church in Africa and Its Evangelizing Mission Towards the Year 2000* (1995), *Ecclesia in America: On the Encounter with the Living Jesus Christ—The Way to Conversion, Communion, and Solidarity in America* (1999), and *Ecclesia in Asia: On Jesus Christ the Savior and His Mission of Love and Service in Asia—"... That They May Have Life, and Have It Abundantly (John 10:10)"* (1999). Other texts will be used as well, in order to reinforce the numerous capacities within which the bishops have endeavored to lead the faithful around the globe according to Christ's expectations in the Gospel.

The International Character of the Church

The Catholic Church has always maintained a distinctly *international* character, as in the precise significance of the term: being *between/among nations*. Hence, Catholicism has never held borders between nations, or other types of frontiers, to inhibit the spread of the Gospel, in the interest of Jesus' command just prior to his Ascension, which we deem the "Great Commission":

> ... All power in heaven and on earth has been given to me. Go, therefore, and make disciples of all nations, baptizing them in the name of the Father, and of the Son, and of the Holy Spirit, teaching them to observe all that I have commanded you. And behold, I am with you always, until the end of the age (Matt 28:18b–20).

Note a particularly potent feature of this most pressing of commands from the Lord: *all* nations ... in other words, evangelization has an inherently international scope. Compare Matthew's version of the Great Commission with Mark's version, in which Jesus proclaims, "Go into the whole world ... " (Mark 16:15a), subsequent to what Jesus had commanded earlier in Mark's Gospel, that the Good News had to "first be preached to all the nations" (Mark 10:31b). In Luke's Gospel, the Lord tells his disciples "that repentance, for the forgiveness of sins, would be preached in his name to all the nations, beginning in Jerusalem" (Luke 24:47). Thus, it is from the confines of Jerusalem that the Apostles begin spreading the Gospel to people of every land throughout the first century world.

Now, it must be conceded that the known "world" of the first century AD, from the perspective of the Apostles as they spread the Good News, was not a particularly extensive one by geographic standards, at least compared to today's "world"; after all, the church did not spread far beyond the Roman Empire until the onset of the Middle Ages. It would be a few hundred years more until the dawn of the Age of Exploration brought the faith around the globe. In modern times, the Catholic Church remains an acutely international institution, so let us examine how the bishops have led the faithful to participate in the blessed privilege of forming disciples around the world.

The Bishops and Making Disciples of All Nations

The bishops, for going on two thousand years, have endeavored to bring the Gospel to all lands, indeed, to the peripheries (to rely on the Jesuit charism) of the human experience. Looking at the particular efforts of bishops when it comes to evangelization since the twentieth century, one readily notes that bishops have reinforced the need to introduce the Gospel in a manner ultimately respectful of the cultural elements inherent to a particular group:

> The Church, in order to be able to offer all of them the mystery of salvation and the life brought by God, must implant herself into these groups for the same motive which led Christ to bind himself, in virtue of his Incarnation, to certain social and cultural conditions of those human beings among whom he dwelt.[1]

In this passage from the Vatican II decree *Ad Gentes: On the Mission Activity of the Church*, note the preoccupation with missionary efforts (frankly, international or even local) aimed at *meeting people where they are*, as it were. This evangelical orientation has fortunately served as a foundation for a great deal of the methods that the bishops have encouraged those charged with missionary efforts to adopt in order to afford greater respect to peoples of different backgrounds, cultures, languages, circumstances, and experiences, all drawing them as fellow children of the Almighty to a steadily greater embrace of the Gospel.

Looking at Pope John Paul II's three post-synodal apostolic exhortations on Africa (1995), the Americas (1999), and Asia (1999), the following are three instrumental passages that indicate the church's interest in manifesting the Gospel on a global scale, always bearing in mind that the church is enriched by the contributions of the faithful from around the globe.

Regarding Africa:

> God's redeeming love embraces the whole of humanity, every race, tribe and nation: thus it also embraces all the peoples of Africa. Divine Providence willed that Africa should be present during the Passion of Christ in the person of Simon of Cyrene, forced by the Roman soldiers to help the Lord to carry the Cross (cf. Mark 15:21).[2]

---

1. Paul VI, *Ad Gentes*, 10.
2. John Paul II, *Ecclesia in Africa*, 27.

In effect, John Paul II's reminder about the presence of a person of African descent in the midst of Jesus' Passion draws us to a greater appreciation of Africa's role in salvation history. And this is not even to mention that Jesus spent his earliest days with Mary and Joseph in Egypt (see Matt 2:13–23). Moreover, following Jesus' Ascension, we find the Apostle Philip sharing the Gospel with the Ethiopian eunuch (see Acts 8:26–40), witnessing again the critical role that the African continent has played in church history. It should hardly be startling that in the twenty-first century the church in (sub-Saharan) Africa is experiencing unprecedented growth, and will continue to contribute to the spiritual vitality and robustness of the church far into the foreseeable future.

Regarding the Americas:

> If the Church in America, in fidelity to the Gospel of Christ, intends to walk the path of solidarity, she must devote special attention to those ethnic groups which even today experience discrimination. Every attempt to marginalize the indigenous peoples must be eliminated. This means, first of all, respecting their territories and the pacts made with them; likewise, efforts must be made to satisfy their legitimate social, health, and cultural requirements. And how can we overlook the need for reconciliation between the indigenous peoples and the societies in which they are living?[3]

John Paul II's efforts at fostering reconciliation and healing the wounds that were wrought by various facets of European colonialism were admirable. Moving forward, the church has, as its duty, the encouragement of everyone of good will to learn from the past in order to secure a future in which the recognition of human rights remains a priority. In this passage, and in similar ones, we bear witness to bishops' leadership when it comes to ensuring that the Gospel is always transmitted gently, patiently, and ultimately, charitably.

Regarding Asia:

> Because Jesus was born, lived, died, and rose from the dead in the Holy Land, that small portion of Western Asia

---

3. John Paul II, *Ecclesia in America*, 64.

became a land of promise and hope for all mankind. Jesus knew and loved this land. He made his own the history, the sufferings, and the hopes of its people. He loved its people and embraced their Jewish traditions and heritage. God in fact had long before chosen this people and revealed himself to them in preparation for the Savior's coming. And from this land, through the preaching of the Gospel in the power of the Holy Spirit, the Church went forth to make "disciples of all nations" (Matt 28:19).[4]

John Paul II's proclamation here serves as a reminder of the crucial role that the Asian continent, in this case regarded as encompassing the Middle East, has played in salvation history. The history of the presence of the church in Asia, accompanying Africa alone in terms of the rapid expanse of the faithful in the twenty-first century, is one that is indicative of the Gospel continuing to spread far and wide, on the same trajectory and with the same fervor with which the Apostles first brought the Gospel beyond the confines of Holy Land.

As these examples from John Paul II's three post-synodal apostolic exhortations on Africa, the Americas, and Asia continue to exhibit, the bishops have been formative in leading efforts to serve humanity in various realms. This leadership, imbued with service, is reflective of Christ's servant leadership: "Just so, the Son of Man did not come to be served but to serve . . . " (Matt 20:28a). Still, geographically speaking, Rome still remains the center of the global church, and we will now examine the situation of this city that is more than merely a city: it was the testing grounds of the church nearly two thousand years ago. Further reinforcing the church's international scope, we must recognize that it is impossible to ponder the globe without noticing that historical realities are not merely international, for they span regions as well. Take, for instance, this point made by Cardinal George in *God in Action*: "Rome was the capital of an empire with universal pretensions when the Catholic Church was born in one of its more unruly provinces two thousand years ago."[5] Yes, the church has experi-

---

4. John Paul II, *Ecclesia in Asia*, 1.
5. George, *God in Action*, 193–94.

ence at surviving in socio-political cauldrons, with the capital of the Roman Empire—its greatest oppressor up until Constantine issued the Edict of Milan in AD 313—eventually becoming the nucleus of ministerial magnanimity.

The Centrality of Rome

Roman Catholicism. Although the Catholic Church has numerous rites, the Roman Catholic Church is centered in Rome (i.e., technically speaking, the Vatican). The location of Rome is significant, given that it is where both Peter and Paul were martyred around AD 65 in the midst of fostering the faith of the small Christian community there, and where Peter's remains are today—at Saint Peter's Basilica. From Rome, the faith spread far and wide, first within the Roman Empire (both before and after its fall), and then beyond the empire's boundaries, yet again with that international scope. Hence, the designation of "Roman" Catholicism automatically draws us back to the church's earliest era.

The Vatican continues to serve as the headquarters of the global Catholic Church. This may seem like a simplistic statement, but its implications are far-reaching: Catholics have a central place to call "home." The bishops have been instrumental in encouraging Catholics to make pilgrimages to Rome and to see the holy sites from the earliest days of Christendom. As Catholics, we can remain grateful to have a central location from which the pope, the Curia, and the College of Cardinals can serve as the hub of the leadership of the global Catholic Church, ensuring that the faithful can be nourished in a manner that is ultimately fulfilling.

A Note on the College of Cardinals

The College of Cardinals has a critical role as far as the bishops are concerned. Their most important task, of course, is easily acknowledged to be that of electing the new pope. On that note, the cardinals are reflective of the church's international character, and their ministerial efforts shepherding the Catholic flock around the globe take them far deeper into the peripheries of humanity than what would have been imaginable even a century ago.

Pope Francis has continued his predecessors' efforts to orient the College of Cardinals to reflect the church's international character. We can rely on the wise insights and pastoral acumen of the cardinals to continue to lead Catholics around the world.

The Bishops and the New Evangelization on a Global Scale

Well into the twenty-first century, the bishops of the world will continue to foster positive international relations, both politically between nations and ecclesiastically within the church. There are various conflicts around the globe (addressed in turn in other chapters), and the reality is that the church has a unique voice when it comes to furthering policies and fostering situations that are in the best interest of humanity. To close with a fitting remark from former archbishop of Paris, Cardinal Jean-Marie Lustiger: "Not that (the Church) presents herself as a court or universal censor, but she receives from God a light on man and on God from which, in her eyes, man's rights and obligations ensue."[6]

---

6. Missika and Wolton, *Choosing God—Chosen by God*, 352.

9

The Laity and the Universal Call to Holiness

Understanding the Post-Vatican II Dynamic

"For as in one body we have many parts, and all the parts do not have the same function, so we, though many, are one body in Christ and individually parts of one another. Since we have gifts that differ according to the grace given to us, let us exercise them: if prophecy, in proportion to the faith; if ministry, in ministering; if one is a teacher, in teaching; if one exhorts, in exhortation; if one contributes, in generosity; if one is over others, with diligence; if one does acts of mercy, with cheerfulness."

(ROM 12:4–8)

Gone are the days when there is a perception that holiness, sanctity, and righteousness are designations reserved for clergymen and religious brothers and sisters alone. The Second Vatican Council ushered in a new era in which the laity is reminded that we are all called to live virtuously, no matter the circumstances of our particular state in life. This is a reality that the laity is thus called to live every day.

The bishops, especially following the Second Vatican Council, have endeavored to remind the laity of their baptismal promises as they relate to the right way to live, with the considerations of the Gospel underpinning this decision-making process. As such, this chapter will identify the numerous manners in which the bishops have sought to reignite a desire among the laity to invite the Lord into their lives to a greater extent, until he is their ultimate consideration. Whether a layperson is married or single, and whether he or she works in ministry or is in a capacity that serves the public broadly, the call to holiness must be embraced daily.

Lumen Gentium and the Universal Call to Holiness in the Church

Vatican II's dogmatic constitution *Lumen Gentium: On the Church* has the same category of import and relevance to the clergy, religious, and laity alike over fifty years after its appearance in 1964. In order to fathom the broader implications of the document, it is necessary to first look at the prescience with which the document calls us to embrace more seriously the need to foster greater adherence to the life of the church in the interest of bringing greater glory to Christ:

> Since the Church is in Christ like a sacrament or as a sign and instrument both of a very closely knit union with God and of the unity of the whole human race, it desires now to unfold more fully to the faithful of the Church and to the whole world its own inner nature and universal mission. This it intends to do following faithfully the teaching of previous councils. The present-day conditions of the world add greater urgency to this work of the Church so that all men, joined more closely today by various social, technical, and cultural ties, might also attain fuller unity in Christ.[1]

---

1. Paul VI, *Lumen Gentium*, 1.

Lumen Gentium actually dedicates an entire chapter to the "universal call to holiness" that it invites us to consider. Thus, the fifth chapter, "The Universal Call to Holiness in the Church," is the crux of the document insofar as it draws us to not be holy for the sake of following rules, but to view the church's decrees and doctrinal teachings as means of reflecting our love for God: "If you love me, you will keep my commandments" (John 14:15). In terms of how to live this life of faith, *Lumen Gentium* offers the following reminder: "The classes and duties of life are many, but holiness is one—that sanctity which is cultivated by all who are moved by the Spirit of God, and who obey the voice of the Father and worship God the Father in spirit and in truth."[2] Furthermore, keeping in mind our particular gifts and talents that we should use in order to magnify the kingdom of God: "Every person must walk unhesitatingly according to his own personal gifts and duties in the path of living faith, which arouses hope and works through charity."[3]

Lumen Gentium likewise features many reminders from the bishops regarding the critical role that they play in reminding the laity of how the Lord is calling them to holiness. Of course, this is in keeping with recognizing Christ as the head of the church, since he "rules her through the supreme pontiff and the bishops."[4] This is a point that will be revisited in the section on how the bishops model holiness for the laity. However, it is necessary to first examine how *Gaudium et Spes* serves as a complement to *Lumen Gentium*. Both of these Vatican II documents contribute to calling the laity to an increase in holiness, and it is indeed in doing so that they build up the church and, in a significant way, contribute to supporting the clergy and religious—a point to be examined toward the end of this chapter.

---

2. Ibid., 41.
3. Ibid.
4. Ibid., 14.

The Laity and the Universal Call to Holiness

The Significance of Gaudium et Spes

The Vatican II pastoral constitution on the church *Gaudium et Spes* continued the trajectory ushered in by *Lumen Gentium* the year prior during the Second Vatican Council. *Gaudium et Spes*'s focus on the universal call to holiness is similar. Likewise, yet again, we see the multiple angles utilized by the bishops to draw the lay faithful to a more mature and well-developed quest for holiness. Of course, *Gaudium et Spes* is especially considerable insofar as it calls us all to a more profound appreciation for the structure of the church as a whole.

In *Gaudium et Spes*, we are reminded that we are indeed "made by God in a state of holiness,"[5] and that we were likewise given the mandate "to govern the world with justice and holiness."[6] Thus, no matter the situation or circumstances, the laity is called upon to use the resources at their disposal to live lives in accordance with God's plans, which necessarily include our striving for holiness and virtue as the pretext for all our activities. Thus, we must recall Jesus' expectations as they relate to our ultimate priority, which acutely orients us to the kingdom of God in the midst of the multitudinous challenges that accompany the life of the disciple: "Seek first the kingdom of God and his righteousness, and all these things will be given you besides" (Matt 6:33).

A distinct feature of *Gaudium et Spes* is the Second Vatican Council's call for married couples in particular to embrace their universal call to holiness. Note the dignity with which the Council addressed those bound in holy matrimony:

> Therefore, by presenting certain key points of Church doctrine in a clearer light, this sacred synod wishes to offer guidance and support to those Christians and other men who are trying to preserve the holiness and to foster the natural dignity of the married state and its superlative value.[7]

---

5. Paul VI, *Gaudium et Spes*, 13.
6. Ibid., 34.
7. Ibid., 47.

This aspect of marital union will be explored further, both in the last section of this chapter and throughout the next chapter. However, it is important to first consider the call of married couples to sanctity as it relates to the broader factor of our universal call to holiness that is further reinforced once children are placed in the equation: "As a result, with their parents leading the way by example and family prayer, children and indeed everyone gathered around the family hearth will find a readier path to human maturity, salvation, and holiness."[8]

Bishops and the Delineation of Holiness for the Laity

The bishops' attempts to delineate the role of the laity and to subsequently model holiness for the laity have resulted in much fruit for the kingdom of God. Looking at the situation of the church in the post-Vatican II world, there is an increasing need to remind the laity of their critically important role regarding the unique ways that they serve the church. This is especially pertinent when it comes to the laity accepting their role as those who can contribute to bringing the Gospel into the temporal realm in a way that the clergy cannot. As Cardinal Wuerl emphasizes in his 2001 book *The Catholic Way: Faith for Living Today*, written while serving as the bishop of Pittsburgh: "Especially, the laity are called to transform the temporal order, which is their particular domain."[9]

Cardinal Wuerl further emphasizes that the laity comprises most of the faithful within the church, for indeed: "By far, the majority membership in the Church is the vast array of women and men baptized into Christ and confirmed in the gifts of the Spirit."[10] Wuerl goes on to provide examples of how this service within the temporal order can be carried out: "To attend to the temporal order is to care for the goods of life and of the family, for

---

8. Ibid., 48.
9. Wuerl, *The Catholic Way*, 115.
10. Ibid., 116.

culture and business, for the arts and professions, for political and social institutions."[11] Thus, the laity has the capacity and, better said, the inherent responsibility, to use their unique circumstances to contribute to the kingdom of God via manners that invite their fellow man to consider the merits of the Catholic faith, including of course the universal call to holiness, which the church both celebrates and promotes.

Also within *The Catholic Way*, Wuerl makes various allusions to the Vatican II decree *Apostolicam Actuositatem: The Apostolate of the Laity*. It is worthwhile to look into a particular excerpt of *Apostolicam Actuositatem* as it relates to the holiness to which the laity is called, particularly in terms of the roles filled within broader society:

> These [spiritual aids] are to be used by the laity in such a way that while correctly fulfilling their secular duties in the ordinary conditions of life, they do not separate union with Christ from their life but rather performing their work according to God's will they grow in that union. In this way the laity must make progress in holiness in a happy and ready spirit, trying prudently and patiently to overcome difficulties.[12]

The holiness to which the bishops continuously call the laity is based on each layperson's acceptance of his or her responsibility to share the Gospel. This evangelization comes in various forms, but features the commonality of being based on our common baptized state. And part of that condition is making recourse to the four Marks of the Church—that it is one, holy, catholic, and apostolic. Of particular note here is the church's holiness.

In his 2013 book *Faith that Transforms Us: Reflections on the Creed*, Cardinal Wuerl leads us through a reflection of the Nicene Creed and its multiple implications for the faith life of the Catholic. In the last paragraph of the Creed, we find the four Marks of the Church. The church's holiness is a consideration that necessarily involves the role of the laity. After all, the church, even in the

---

11. Ibid.
12. Paul VI, *Apostolicam Actuositatem*, 4.

midst of a hierarchical structure as it relates precisely to the clergy and religious, also has a familial element:

> The Church is a family, a household. Its members see one another as brothers and sisters (Col 1:2). We share a common birth in baptism. We share a common table in the Eucharist. We hold ourselves to a higher standard of care for one another. Our family is identifiable—there is a family resemblance. Our Church bears certain "marks"—visible signs of the invisible Spirit. We say in the Creed that the Church is "one, holy, catholic, and apostolic."[13]

Thus, Cardinal Wuerl draws the laity to remember whom all of the faithful in the church, no matter our specific vocation, are called to be: "[Jesus] made the Church 'a holy nation' (1 Pet 2:9). Its members on earth, though sinners, are called to be 'holy ones,' or saints (Col 1:2)."[14]

The Bishops, Married Couples, and Living Holiness in the Twenty-First Century World

Beyond the Second Vatican Council, the bishops have continued to look for opportunities to instill in the laity a greater appreciation for the need for holiness in all aspects of life. This is especially pertinent in the case of married couples, a topic that will be explored at even greater depth in the next chapter. No doubt, there are challenges that come with endeavoring to embrace holiness, even (or, as the more inveterate may consider, *especially*) in married life. However, with the encouragement of the bishops, the married laity will only benefit spiritually from a greater respect for the Lord's wishes to see them living according to his divine will, in the interest of their ultimate wellbeing.

The reality is that married couples striving to live the Good News faithfully need the bishops now more than ever, in order to encourage and support them as they aim for holiness as they

---

13. Wuerl, *Faith that Transforms Us*, 101.
14. Ibid., 103.

The Laity and the Universal Call to Holiness

endeavor to bring Christ into the world, beginning with the privileged duty of raising their children in the domestic church of their homes. Pope Benedict XVI, in an exemplary way, places the matter in perspective in order to emphasize what is at stake, via his 2009 book *The Joy of Knowing Christ: Meditations on the Gospels*:

> My thoughts now go to all Christian spouses: I thank the Lord with them for the gift of the Sacrament of Marriage, and I urge them to remain faithful to their vocation in every season of life, "in good times and in bad, in sickness and in health," as they promised in the sacramental rite. Conscious of the grace that they have received, may Christian husbands and wives build a family open to life and capable of facing united the many complex challenges of our time.[15]

Thus, to close, just as Cardinal Wuerl discusses in *Faith that Transforms Us*, in consideration of the Nicene Creed and the four Marks of the Church, Pope Benedict XVI reminds us later in *The Joy of Knowing Christ* of how the collective church community can continually quest for the holiness to which we are all called, independent of our state in life: "The Church is *holy*, not by her own merits, but because, animated by the Holy Spirit, she keeps her gaze on Christ, to become conformed to him and his love."[16]

---

15. Benedict XVI, *The Joy of Knowing Christ*, 100–101.
16. Ibid., 139.

10

Marriage, the Family, and the Gift of Children

Promoting a Sacred Institution and the Foundation of Society

"[Jesus] said in reply, 'Have you not read that from the beginning the Creator "made them male and female" and said, "For this reason a man shall leave his father and mother and be joined to his wife, and the two shall become one flesh"? So they are no longer two, but one flesh. Therefore, what God has joined together, no human being must separate.'"

(MATT 19:4–6)

As an indicator of the true beauty of marriage as a covenantal bond between a husband and wife, an effective manner that the bishops have employed to promote the sacrament of holy matrimony is to underscore its unitive characteristics. In this approach, the bishops have been able to promote the sanctifying qualities of good, holy marriages without coming off as pretentiously anachronistic in the face of a society that is perhaps less inclined toward marriage than previous generations. Thus, the truth and goodness inherent to the sacrament of matrimony will continue to flourish, and with them being applauded, their beauty will continue to be evidenced.

In these times, just as in past eras, it is vital for Catholics to be able to articulate the church's teachings on marriage, which have been underscored and ardently defended by the bishops. This accentuation of the true beauty of the sacrament of holy matrimony is likewise an expectation for the Catholic faithful in light of the New Evangelization. The task of encouraging society to recognize holy marriages in the spirit of the New Evangelization is not necessarily an easy one, for as Cardinal Wuerl reminds us in *Seek First the Kingdom*, "The ground may be rocky, filled with thorns, or heavily trafficked by human feet, but each and every Catholic can make a difference. This is the New Evangelization."[1]

The valor with which our bishops have encouraged men and women to seek sanctity within marriage is commendable and, as such, this sacrament of the union of husband and wife has endured and prospered in light of "its institution and the meaning God has given it."[2] Focusing on the polemics presented by the twenty-first century, fraught with various challenges to the expectations and implications of holy matrimony, the modern bishops have repeatedly collaborated on how to best explain the church's celebration of the sacred institution of marriage.

The Bishops' Emphasis on the Sacred Covenant of Marriage

The work of such bishops' committees as the USCCB's Committee on Laity, Marriage, Family Life, and Youth has been significant in terms of the results of their labors to highlight the extensively rewarding contributions of the sacrament of matrimony to humanity, ultimately orienting marriage to the kingdom of God. Due

---

1. Wuerl, *Seek First the Kingdom*, 177.
2. *Catechism of the Catholic Church*, 1602.

emphasis is therefore placed on the reality of the sanctifying nature of matrimony as a *sacrament*, i.e., that which is *sacred*, or "set apart." This understanding of the critical nature of the church's teaching is particularly noticeable in the endeavors of such initiatives as the USCCB's Subcommittee for the Promotion and Defense of Marriage. In fact, one of the Subcommittee members, Archbishop Salvatore Cordileone of the Archdiocese of San Francisco, reminded us of the following during his homily titled "Married Love and the Transformation of the Human by the Divine" at a mass for wedding anniversaries on February 21, 2015: "This sacrificial self-offering between husband and wife is at the heart of every marriage, but our faith teaches us that in Christian marriage this sacrifice is also a sacrament."[3] Hence, Archbishop Cordileone has effectively underscored the sacramental nature of holy matrimony by providing the correlation between *sacrifice* and *sacrament*.

During his pontificate, and both before and throughout his service as the Prefect of the Congregation for the Doctrine of the Faith as Cardinal Joseph Ratzinger, Benedict XVI likewise underscored the beautiful sacramental bond inherent to marriage. Benedict used various opportunities to emphasize the role of marriage as an expression of our covenantal relationship with God. So special was the sacrament of matrimony to Pope Benedict's explications of what is understood by the profound theological concept of *love* that, in 2005, he delved into the sacramental nature of marriage within the framework of his first encyclical, *Deus Caritas Est*, as seen in the section titled "The Newness of Biblical Faith":

> From the standpoint of creation, *eros* directs man towards marriage, to a bond which is unique and definitive; thus, and only thus, does it fulfill its deepest purpose. Corresponding to the image of a monotheistic God is monogamous marriage. Marriage based on exclusive and definitive love becomes the icon of the relationship between God and his people and vice versa.[4]

---

3. Cordileone, "Married Love and the Transformation of the Human by the Divine," 2.

4. Benedict XVI, *Deus Caritas Est*, 11.

Marriage, the Family, and the Gift of Children

The Bishops and Continuity from Benedict XVI to Francis

Similarly to Pope Benedict XVI, Pope Francis, soon after being elevated to the papacy, used the opportunity of his first major papal document, *Lumen Fidei*, to emphasize the complementary nature of husband and wife united in holy matrimony. Under the section "Faith and the Family," Pope Francis reminds us of the divine orientation of the sacrament of matrimony. (Read the excerpt from paragraph 52 of *Lumen Fidei* within the chapter on human sexuality, under the heading "The Bishops' Emphasis on the Complementary Nature of Man and Woman.")

In the same manner by which Pope Benedict XVI and Pope Francis used the occasion of such writings as papal encyclicals to address the theological underpinnings of the sacrament of marriage, so too have numerous bishops highlighted the many positive elements of marriage in considerably prominent ways, casting light upon the public nature of this sacrament of creative unity. In June 2014, Cardinal Wuerl held a mass to honor over eight-hundred couples from across the Archdiocese of Washington who were celebrating milestone wedding anniversaries. Within the context of the mass, Cardinal Wuerl not only led the couples in the renewal of their vows; he also reminded them of their ultimate significance, as we read in this excerpt from the news report provided by the Archdiocese of Washington:

> "In you whose jubilees we celebrate today, we recognize the power of God's Spirit at work," said Cardinal Wuerl in his homily. "It is manifested in your love for each other. In the promises you made to be true to each other in good times and in bad, in sickness and in health, that you would love and honor each other all the days of your life, you accepted to do your part in what Jesus asked of you—to be his witness to his Gospel, his love, and the transforming power of his Spirit in this world."[5]

---

5. Archdiocese of Washington, "Cardinal Wuerl Honors More Than 800 Couples Celebrating Milestone Anniversaries," June 15, 2014.

Highlighting the task of the New Evangelization, Cardinal Wuerl went on to comment on the role of matrimony within the overall framework of the promotion of the Gospel when he reminded those present that, "We are asked to see in your married life, in the jubilee we celebrate today, a work of the New Evangelization. Your lives are a testimony to the power of God's grace at work in you."[6]

Addressing the Challenges to Marriage with Charity

Returning to the efforts of such conferences as the USCCB, the bishops have vigorously articulated the church's position on marriage in a fashion that is at once truthful, charitable, and sensitive. In the comprehensive 2009 pastoral letter, *Marriage: Love and Life in the Divine Plan*, the USCCB's Committee on Laity, Marriage, Family Life, and Youth explains the complementary nature of husband and wife within marriage, along with the two essential elements of marriage: that it is *unitive* and *procreative*. The document goes on to address the "Fundamental Challenges to the Nature and Purpose of Marriage,"[7] and how it is critical for both the clergy, religious, and laity to be able to understand how to assist those who are dealing with particular circumstances of life. An important feature of *Marriage: Love and Life in the Divine Plan* is the way that the bishops who were involved, typical of their role as our pastoral leaders, discussed these topics with not only factual evidence, ecclesial wisdom, and moral clarity, but likewise, with exceptional sensitivity and supportive encouragement for the Christian moral perseverance of those struggling with how to "take up [their] cross daily and follow [Jesus]" (Luke 9:23).

A readily apparent reality of modern times is that the bishops have had to both preach and clarify the church's enduring teachings on the sanctity of marriage. This preaching, both in spoken

---

6. Ibid.
7. United States Conference of Catholic Bishops, *Marriage*, 17–28.

and written word, has been based on their charitable pastoral role. Likewise, this clarification of church teachings has required them to utilize profound theological concepts in order to engage society in a dialogue that is necessarily undergirded by a religious viewpoint in matters related to the divine orientation of the sacrament of marriage. Given the reality of these two practices of preaching and clarifying that bishops have had to employ, it is worthwhile to note the adeptness with which they have had to underscore how authentic Christian moral principles regarding the sanctity of marriage are ultimately charitable, in that they are in accord with the fullness of divine love and stand at the very core of the foundations of an ultimately functional society.

Returning to our coverage of how bishops, within the scope of the New Evangelization, have underscored what marriage is, it is vital to enter into a discussion of how bishops have professed and emphasized the numerous ways in which Christian marriage is markedly beneficial for society. This consideration is particularly relevant when we view the Holy Family as our model for sanctity. Of course, the Holy Family is the archetype for familial sacredness and unity, so it would be impossible for us to emulate their divine dynamic. Nonetheless, we are called to imitate the courage with which Mary and Joseph guarded and protected the Lord Jesus Christ during his youth and formative segments of his earthly reign, playing their critical role within salvation history in order to essentially serve the kingdom of God.

Yet another reminder from the bishops of the important role that marriage plays in society came in the form of a communiqué from the Catholic Bishops' Conference of Nigeria at the end of their first plenary meeting, February 20–26, 2015. The Nigerian bishops had the opportunity to remind the faithful of the distinctive role that the family, in due consideration of the relational dynamics of the husband, wife, and their children, plays within broader society:

> The family is at the service of love and life when parents educate their children on the essential values of human life—to love the truth, to love the good, to love and to

be loved, to love God. This is itself the ministry of the Church in which the family is able to participate when husband and wife live in fidelity, love, and mutual respect. In this way, parents teach their children to love in the wider society, and good families build good nations.[8]

The bishops of Nigeria went on to encourage married couples to persevere in their vocation to holy matrimony by recalling how this covenantal Christian bond is a distinctive reflection of God's love for us, and one that likewise fosters faithful education for future generations: "In our need to restore family values, let husband and wife mirror the love of God to each other. By their example as parents, let them be the first and the best teachers to their children."[9]

Supporting Married Couples in the Twenty-First Century

As the church continues well into the twenty-first century, the bishops will continue to support and promote the beauty of marriage and the family. As alluded to previously, the bishops will likewise continue to profess the church's timeless teaching on the uniqueness of the sacrament while ensuring that they speak charity in truth to those who may feel drawn away from living based on the church's moral teachings. In the spirit of this Gospel-driven charity, the Catholic bishops of England and Wales issued a December 2014 joint pastoral letter titled *The Call, the Journey, and the Mission: An Invitation from the Bishops of England and Wales to Reflect on the Gift of Marriage and Family Life*. In this document, the English and Welsh bishops succinctly and effectively reminded us of some key terms regarding what marriage truly is: a *call*, a *journey*, a *mission*, a *gift*, and a sacrament intended for *family life*.[10]

---

8. Vatican Radio, "Nigerian Catholic Bishops: Good Families Make Good Nations," February 26, 2015.

9. Ibid.

10. Catholic Bishops of England and Wales, *The Call, the Journey, and the Mission*, 1.

Ultimately, our Catholic bishops have shown us that God's love must form the foundation of a solid marriage. In his timeless classic, *Three to Get Married: An Inspiring Guide to Love and Marriage*, Venerable Archbishop Fulton Sheen reminds us that "When one reads of the tremendous transformation of souls in the Sacrament of Matrimony, one realizes that through them, as well as in a life specifically ascetic and detached, such as in the monastery and the cloister, there can be born a fiery and ardent love of God."[11] May all married couples, based on the supreme model and powerful intercession of the Holy Family, continue to live that wonderful dynamic of husband and wife that allows them to yearn for this *fiery and ardent love of God*, as posited by Sheen. With the continued labors of our bishops in teaching the truth of the beauty of Christ-centered marriages, the sacrament of matrimony will continue to serve as an ideal framework for spouses to lead each other to a life in Christ while remaining open to raising children for the greater glory of the kingdom of God.

---

11. Sheen, *Three to Get Married*, 303.

11

Persecution of the Global Church
Living as "Sheep in the Midst of Wolves"

"Behold, I am sending you like sheep in the midst of wolves . . . You will be hated by all because of my name, but whoever endures to the end will be saved . . . No disciple is above his teacher, no slave above his master. It is enough for the disciple that he become like his teacher, for the slave that he become like his master. If they have called the master of the house Beelzebul, how much more those of his household!"

(MATT 10:16, 22, 24–25)

The above passage, which appears in all three Synoptic Gospels, is the excerpted Matthean version of what has been deemed the "Coming Persecutions," as it is likewise deemed within the Marcan version (13:9–13) and the Lucan version (21:12–19). It is advised that the reader prayerfully and patiently read through these three accounts in their entirety, in order to better fathom their implication, especially as it relates to the circumstances of Christians—both Catholics and many other Christian groups—around the world. For now, it is worthwhile to read Matthew's version of Jesus' call for the fortitude that is expected of his disciples in the midst of this oppression of Christians:

> "Therefore do not be afraid of them. Nothing is concealed that will not be revealed, nor secret that will not be known. What I say to you in the darkness, speak in the light; what you hear whispered, proclaim on the housetops. And do not be afraid of those who kill the body but cannot kill the soul; rather, be afraid of the one who can destroy both soul and body in Gehenna. Are not two sparrows sold for a small coin? Yet not one of them falls to the ground without your Father's knowledge. Even all the hairs of your head are counted. So do not be afraid; you are worth more than many sparrows. Everyone who acknowledges me before others I will acknowledge before my heavenly Father. But whoever denies me before others, I will deny before my heavenly Father." (Matt 10:26–33)

Reflecting on this situation within the Gospels, it is crucial for the Christian to bear in mind that there has never been an "easy" time to be a disciple of Jesus Christ, even during the expansive epoch of "Christendom" (as we see in the cases of Saint Joan of Arc, Saint Teresa of Ávila, Saint John of the Cross, and other now-prominently celebrated canonized saints whose personal sanctity in the midst of their apostolates did not prevent them from falling out of favor even within the localized ecclesial structures of their time).

The quandary of Christians around the world is one that is rife with difficulties due to suppression at least and martyrdom-laden oppression at most, in many realms of the globe. Extremist terrorist groups, increasingly secularizing—if not outright atheistic—governmental structures, legal martyrdom by anti-Christian political action, and other threats are posed to Christians worldwide. Some examples of these circumstances were already presented in the chapter on the church in the public square. The bishops have served heroically as they endeavor to lead their global flock as faithful shepherds opposing the menacing presence of the wolves comprised of multiple different forms and appearances bent on impeding the presence and influence of Christianity worldwide.

The Bishops, the Church, and Respect for Other Faiths

There are sometimes claims that the church is intolerant of other faiths. However, the reality could not be more distant from the accusation. One need but look at such monumental documents as the Vatican II declaration *Nostra Aetate: On the Relation of the Church to Non-Christian Religions* in order to fathom the leadership role that the Catholic Church has adopted since the twenty-first century when it comes to enabling, facilitating, and promoting interreligious dialogue. Note, for example, how the following excerpt underscores what the church expects of the Catholic faithful when it comes to recognizing the importance of fostering good will among those of other faith traditions:

> The Church, therefore, exhorts her sons, that through dialogue and collaboration with the followers of other religions, carried out with prudence and love and in witness to the Christian faith and life, they recognize, preserve, and promote the good things, spiritual and moral, as well as the socio-cultural values found among these men.[1]

As seen in this excerpt from *Nostra Aetate*, it is a fundamental expectation of Catholics to respect the shared human dignity of those of other faith traditions. This in no way is intended to imply that Catholics can compromise our own teachings and beliefs, but this assertion is in keeping with the Lord's expectations that evangelization is always an invitation, and never an imposition: "Behold, I stand at the door and knock. If anyone hears my voice and opens the door, then I will enter his house and dine with him, and he with me" (Rev 3:20).

Unfortunately, there have been occasions—both isolated and systematically condoned—when some prominent figures within the Catholic Church attempted to force others to convert to Catholicism. Each of these situations must be evaluated individually and within its accurate context, and many of these offenses accompanied injustices that those individuals responsible were already

---

1. Paul VI, *Nostra Aetate*, 2.

carrying out, although this hardly constitutes any type of excuse. At the same time, it must be offered that, from a Catholic perspective, the faith can never be justifiably imparted through actual violence, threats of violence, or any other type of coercion, lest we neglect Jesus' stark position on the matter:

> "Not everyone who says to me, 'Lord, Lord,' will enter the kingdom of heaven, but only the one who does the will of my Father in heaven. Many will say to me on that day, 'Lord, Lord, did we not prophesy in your name? Did we not drive out demons in your name? Did we not do mighty deeds in your name?' Then I will declare to them solemnly, 'I never knew you. Depart from me, you evildoers.'" (Matt 7:21–23)

Thus, the church cannot stand for any category of malice or ill will against any member of any other faith community. Quite the opposite, in line with *Nostra Aetate*, the church is called to recognize the inalienable value of every other member of our human family, regardless of his or her religious affiliation. Would that those of other mainstream faiths, in nations and communities around the globe, afford the same category of respect to those who follow the peace-laden commands of Jesus. Unfortunately, this is not always the outcome, and this is what the bishops have addressed in the past few decades in particular, especially when confronted with the menace of extremist violence and terrorist attacks that have been on the rise around the globe.

Persecution of Christians by Extremist Religious Groups

In the chapter on ecumenism and interreligious dialogue, we observed how figures such as Cardinal Francis Arinze of Nigeria have fostered positive relations between Catholics and those of other faith communities. However, what happens when there are groups who are intolerant of Christians and others who do not ascribe to their ideologies? Cardinal Arinze, in *Meeting Other Believers: The Risks and Rewards of Interreligious Dialogue*, identifies the setting that typifies religious extremism, which serves as kindling to the infernal elements of terrorism:

> More than one country is troubled by religious extremists. These are people who, in their desire to be faithful to what they consider to be the original and undiluted form of their religion, adopt extreme measures toward other believers, or even toward the more moderate members of their own religious community. They, for example, want all religions to be illegal in their country except their own religion, and to promote this they are ready even to kill.[2]

Cardinal Arinze goes on to emphasize the preoccupation experienced by those of good will, including those of different faith communities: "All genuine religious leaders, as well as thoughtful civil authorities, are worried by the phenomenon of religious extremism."[3] It is worthwhile to note that Cardinal Arinze wrote this book in 1998, just years before global terrorism became that much more of a reality following the jihadist terrorist group Al Qaeda's attacks in New York, Pennsylvania, and Virginia on the morning of September 11, 2001.

Subsequently, in his 2002 book, *Religions for Peace: A Call for Solidarity to the Religions of the World*, Arinze offers the following, which juxtaposes the dynamics of extremist violence carried out under the banner of certain mainstream faiths across history, beginning by admitting the errors that various (read: hardly all) crusaders committed long ago as far as church history is concerned:

> People of religions, however, should go carefully and not be too quick to declare themselves innocent and other people guilty of any ensuing violence. The desire of the originators of the Crusades, for example, may have been blameless and religiously acceptable: to get back the Holy Places sanctified by the life, suffering, and death of Jesus Christ. But that does not mean that everything de facto done by the crusaders is to be approved. A Muslim may be blameless in desiring to share his religion with others.

2. Arinze, *Meeting Other Believers*, 31.
3. Ibid.

But it is quite another matter what means he uses to spread that conviction. Force, violence, destruction, and conquest cannot be approved.[4]

Of course, any faithful person of truly good will must concede that generalizations cannot, and should not, carry weight in today's pluralistic world, and broad categorizations of entire groups of people are summarily unjustified. Nevertheless, simultaneously, Cardinal Arinze and other bishops have had to identify and call to task, by name, certain extremist groups who have openly professed their desire to intimidate, if not unequivocally blast away, any manifestation of the "People of the Cross" in their midst. As such, in accord with the prudence and wisdom of Cardinal Arinze, other Catholic bishops have endeavored to promote peace, justice, and a call to conversion of heart in the face of religious extremist groups such as Al Qaeda, Boko Haram, ISIS, and other jihadist affiliates and their backers. Bishops have supported such Catholic organizations as Aid to the Church in Need, the Knights of Columbus, and others who have furthered global efforts to bring attention to the plight of Christians threatened by religious extremists. Note, for instance, that it was the Knights of Columbus' 280-page report titled *Genocide against Christians in the Middle East*, submitted to the United States Secretary of State John Kerry in March 2016, that finally led the State Department to declare that ISIS's systematic massacre of Christians in the Middle East had reached genocidal proportions.[5]

Looking to the bishops of the Middle East provides examples of the courage that bishops have shown in not simply opposing terrorist groups, but in offering substantive hope to their faithful flocks, who are in many circumstances simply trying to survive against all odds. Further examining the contributions of groups such as the Knights of Columbus, consider these words of hope and fortitude extended to Supreme Knight Carl Anderson and the Knights of Columbus by Archbishop Bashar Matti Warda, CSsR, of the Chaldean Archdiocese of Erbil, Iraq:

4. Arinze, *Religions for Peace*, 34–35.
5. Knights of Columbus, "Knights of Columbus Provides Major Report on Genocide of Christians to State Department," March 10, 2016.

> We remain confident in Christ that there is a future for Iraqi Christians in Iraq. Even as we work to meet the absolutely urgent need of our people for shelter, we are working hard to build schools and medical facilities which will provide services to the community at large, economic prosperity, and an environment where the face of Christ is reflected in the smiles and hearts of all Iraqis.[6]

Bishops Aspiring for More Tolerance of Christianity in the Twenty-First Century

There are multiple additional examples of bishops who have courageously embraced the Gospel in the face of religiously motivated terrorism, come what may. Archbishop Jean-Clement Jeanbart of Aleppo, Syria, has faithfully led his flock in the midst of terror, civil war, and the humanitarian nightmare that is the intersection thereof, providing this stark assessment of ISIS's intent, likewise in the context of a letter to Carl Anderson: "Allow me to raise my voice to call on all men and women of good will to hear our plea. ISIS, which has already killed thousands in the region, is terrifying the faithful of Aleppo."[7] Bishop Oliver Doeme, of the Diocese of Maiduguri in northeastern Nigeria, has encouraged his faithful to pray the Rosary to combat the onslaught of Boko Haram, seemingly with positive outcomes.[8] Multiple such examples abound.

Pope Francis has reliably been the sole world leader interested in underscoring the plight of Christians around the globe. There are numerous hotbeds for intolerance of Christianity, not to mention of other mainstream faiths, including North Korea, Somalia, Yemen, and other areas where the Gospel is viewed as anything other than the Good News. Nonetheless, Christians

---

6. Warda, "Letter to Carl Anderson and the Knights of Columbus," May 8, 2015, 2.

7. Jeanbart, "Letter to Carl Anderson and the Knights of Columbus," May 27, 2015, 2.

8. *National Catholic Register*, "Nigerian Bishop Doeme Combats Boko Haram with 'Rosary Battle Plan,'" October 12, 2016.

continue to propose this enduring Good News, sometimes earning the crown of martyrdom as a result. Thus, how fitting are the words of Pope Francis from within his 2013 apostolic exhortation *Evangelii Gaudium: On the Proclamation of the Gospel in Today's World*: "The disciple is ready to put his or her whole life on the line, even to accepting martyrdom, in bearing witness to Jesus Christ, yet the goal is not to make enemies but to see God's word accepted and its capacity for liberation and renewal revealed."[9]

The Catholic bishops will surely continue to serve as leaders, joining others of good will in vocally and substantively opposing the global persecution of Christians. The laity would do well to continue to gain inspiration from the bishops' words of hope that they have offered. An example of such a resource is Cardinal Wuerl's 2015 book *To the Martyrs: A Reflection on the Supreme Christian Witness*. Let us thus heed Cardinal Wuerl's hope-imbued advice: "Let us act, so that no one may say that we lack hope. Even in the face of these outrages, we believe in the power of prayer and we know that God's grace can touch and change every human heart."[10] Indeed, it is far from a cliché statement to affirm that love will always conquer in the end. After all, although previous eras featured significant, sometimes even sanguine, discord between Christian groups themselves, the twenty-first century affords Christians of all different affiliations—Catholics and others alike—the opportunity to redouble our efforts to speak out against the injustice of religious intolerance in its manifold forms, showing the world what believers in Jesus Christ have to offer: "I give you a new commandment: love one another. As I have loved you, so you also should love one another" (John 13:35).

---

9. Francis, *Evangelii Gaudium*, 24.
10. Wuerl, *To the Martyrs*, 105.

12

The Poor and Vulnerable
Serving Christ in Our Midst

"Do not store up for yourselves treasures on earth, where moth and decay destroy, and thieves break in and steal. But store up treasures in heaven, where neither moth nor decay destroys, nor thieves break in and steal. For where your treasure is, there also will your heart be."

(MATT 6:19–21)

The contributions of the bishops to alleviating the plight of those suffering under the yoke of poverty can hardly be overestimated. Over the course of the last approximately two centuries in particular, especially in consideration of the Industrial Revolution and the advent of globalization, the church has taken an increasingly active role in underscoring the need to extend unrelenting service to those whom material destitution has ravaged. At the same time, the church has emphasized the need to address those mired in spiritual poverty, a dire ailment of personal resolve that is as widespread as it is enduringly deleterious to the condition of the soul.

The bishops have taken up the charge to lead the church to embrace the Gospel insofar as it mandates that we serve those living in poverty. Indeed, in doing so, we are further drawn to fathom whom we are ultimately serving: "And the king will say to them in reply, 'Amen, I say to you, whatever you did for one of these least brothers of mine, you did for me'" (Matt 25:40). The writings of the bishops over the last approximately one hundred and twenty-five years, especially in the wake of the Industrial Revolution that swept through the nations of the global West as of the early 1800s, reflect the seriousness with which they have responded to the call to serve those living in poverty. Thus, a good place to begin covering this matter is to examine the contributions of Pope Leo XIII by way of his 1891 encyclical *Rerum Novarum: On Capital and Labor*.

The Momentousness of Pope Leo XIII's Rerum Novarum

Rerum Novarum was a watershed moment in the Catholic Church's call to live the Christian principles inherent to social justice. This is not to say that prior to *Rerum Novarum*, the church was not committed to serving those in poverty. After all, since the days of the early church, faithful bishops have reminded their flock of the importance of caring for the needy in their midst. One need but look at figures such as Saint Nicholas of Myra (270–343), that great charity-imbued bishop from modern-day Turkey, whom secular society has notoriously transmogrified into the perennial epitome of a purveyor of materialistic consumerism, in order to recognize how bishops have been devoted to mollifying the conditions of the disadvantaged. Unfortunately, within the span of nearly two millennia, not every prelate has had such an interest. Nevertheless, multiple examples of those who have are ready in abundance.

What made *Rerum Novarum* unique is that Leo XIII both calls on the faithful to recognize the human rights that are inherent to the worker, and also reminds us that the duty to serve those living in harsh conditions is not simply the expectation of governmental systems, but must also include the full scope of charity that is indicative of the Gospel. Leo XIII indicates the prescience of the matter, given the global circumstances of the late nineteenth century that occasioned the necessity of such a pertinent reminder: "In any case we clearly see, and on this there is general agreement, that some opportune remedy must be found quickly for the misery and wretchedness pressing so unjustly on the majority of the working class...."[1]

Rerum Novarum reasserts the church's commitment to serving those mired in material poverty. By reaffirming the church's responsibility—really, a *privilege*—to underscore the value of every single human being, Leo XIII ushered in a new era in the church's dedication to seeing the face of Christ in the poor, and to inviting those in all conditions to raise up their fellow man, steadily bringing him closer to the Lord. Of course, as Leo XIII has posited, and as bishops since him have reiterated, the matter must always be framed within the context of the Good News: "God himself seems to incline rather to those who suffer misfortune; for Jesus Christ calls the poor 'blessed' (Matt 5:3); he lovingly invites those in labor and grief to come to him for solace (Matt 11:28); and he displays the tenderest charity toward the lowly and the oppressed."[2]

Poverty and the Catholic Church in the United States

A tome could be spent detailing the economic might of the United States, and indeed, there are already numerous resources evidencing the prominent role of the United States in the global economy. This reality arose most markedly in the twentieth century, and even in the midst of the financial challenges to world markets in the twenty-first century, the United States remains a commercial powerhouse. The United States has a distinct opportunity to continue serving those who are living in poverty, both within the United States and around the globe. The bishops of the United States have

1. Leo XIII, *Rerum Novarum*, 3.
2. Ibid., 24.

called on both citizens and public servants to look for opportunities to serve the homeless, hungry, and otherwise impoverished in our midst. The following are a few examples of documents that have shown the bishops' commitment to stressing the dignity of all people in all circumstances, particularly the poor and vulnerable.

The United States Conference of Catholic Bishops' 1986 document *Economic Justice for All: Pastoral Letter on Catholic Social Teaching and the U.S. Economy*, while over thirty years old at this point, contains numerous points that are just as relevant within the economic situation of the twenty-first century. *Economic Justice for All* invites the Catholic faithful to a greater embrace of the social doctrine of the church as it relates to how to most effectively serve those living in poverty. The challenging situations that *Economic Justice for All* identifies include the wide gap between the materially rich and the materially poor, the dilemmas faced in modern American society, threats to justice broadly speaking, and other polemics that must be evaluated from a Christian viewpoint. A theme that courses through *Economic Justice for All* is how we preserve our human dignity, no matter our economic status: "The basis for all that the Church believes about the moral dimensions of economic life is its vision of the transcendent worth—the sacredness—of human beings."[3] It is advisable that the faithful in the twenty-first century read *Economic Justice for All* carefully and prayerfully, especially at this juncture in history, when economic inequality is a daily reality for so many.

In the decades following *Economic Justice for All*, other Catholic bishops in the United States have taken up the task of offering responses to the dilemma of poverty that include both temporal remedies and the requirement that we continue to place the matter within the broader context of the Gospel, based on Christ's expectations of service within our communities. One such example is the 2012 *Who Is My Neighbor?: A Pastoral Letter on the Occasion of National Poverty Awareness Month*, by Bishop George Murry, SJ, of the Diocese of Youngstown, Ohio. In *Who Is My Neighbor?*, Bishop Murry reminds us that poverty is a reality that many face every

---

3. United States Conference of Catholic Bishops, *Economic Justice for All*, 28.

single day, and just as his fellow bishops posit in *Economic Justice for All*, Bishop Murry extends his message in line with the scriptural affirmation that we all reflect God's glory: "One fundamental insight from Scripture forms the functional understanding of the Church: despite one's economic, social, or immigration status, every person is created in the image and likeness of God. Consequently, every person possesses a dignity that requires respect."[4] Also in 2012, Bishop Michael Bransfield of the Diocese of Wheeling-Charleston issued *Setting Children Free: Loosening the Bonds of Poverty in West Virginia: A Pastoral Letter*. In this sweeping pastoral letter, Bishop Bransfield reminds us that the call to serve those living in poverty is a call that all Catholics must take up personally, because such is our expectation as disciples of Christ:

> It is my hope to speak to the grief and anguish of the poor among us, especially the experience of our children and families in poverty, and offer to them a compassionate message of joy and hope. At the same time, I want to invite you, dear brothers and sisters, to join me in compassionate care for the poor and continual solicitude on their behalf.[5]

The hope is that the American bishops will continue to participate in this call to serve those living in poverty. Of course, this is only one dimension. It is crucial to look at what is going on beyond the United States as well, in order to see that service to the poor is important for the global church to continue to put into practice, for the greater glory of the kingdom of God.

Other Emblematic Responses to Global Poverty by Bishops

In 1996, the Canadian Conference of Catholic Bishops issued *The Struggle Against Poverty: A Sign of Hope in Our World—Pastoral Letter by the Episcopal Commission for Social Affairs on the Elimination of Poverty*. A segment of the text is fitting insofar as it draws

---

4. Murry, *Who Is My Neighbor?*, 5.
5. Bransfield, *Setting Children Free*, 2.

us to a more profound comprehension of what is at the root of many categories of material poverty:

> Material poverty is not necessarily a permanent situation, nor is it intrinsically negative. It is not a personal problem of certain "unworthy" individuals. Poverty is sometimes caused by environmental factors or by private or public corruption. Poverty may also be the result of illness, disability, or simply the lack of personal initiative. Most often, however, poverty is the result of economic processes created and directed by humans. Viewed in this light, poverty appears as a phenomenon that we can influence. We can change such processes by making different societal choices.[6]

This particular excerpt from the Canadian bishops' pastoral letter has implications for what we continue to see around the globe twenty years later. In the next section on the contributions of various recent popes to combating the devastating effects of poverty, those implications remain evident. For now, let us look at a few considerations regarding the state of the church as it continues to seek ways to combat poverty in Africa, Asia, and Latin America in particular. The writings of the great global traveler, Saint John Paul II, serve as our frame of reference here.

Many regions of Africa are mired in poverty, and hunger in these areas is rampant. There are many places where abject poverty is the norm, rather than the exception. The scope of this book does not provide for particular case studies in the obstacles that certain regions face, but as Saint John Paul II notes in *Ecclesia in Africa*, the church's role in fomenting collaborative efforts is critical: "In spite of its poverty and the meager means at its disposal, the Church in Africa plays a leading role in what touches upon integral human development. Its remarkable achievements in this regard are often recognized by governments and international experts."[7]

The church in Asia likewise undertakes such collaborative efforts. This is even in light of the precarious economic situations

---

6. Canadian Conference of Catholic Bishops, *The Struggle Against Poverty*, I.
7. John Paul II, *Ecclesia in Africa*, 45.

of various Asian countries. Thus, regarding some specific regional concerns within Asia, John Paul II notes in *Ecclesia in Asia* that, "the persistent reality of poverty and the exploitation of people are matters of the most urgent concern."[8]

The church in Latin America has its own set of challenges in terms of appropriately addressing poverty. There is some overlap in terms of the manifold causes of poverty. However, there are likewise unique regional considerations. Again, John Paul II calls on the church to continue to use its role within society to lift up those who are downtrodden and in misery, especially based on aggressive human action: "The particular Churches in America must raise a prophetic voice to condemn the arms race and the scandalous arms trade, which consumes huge sums of money which should instead be used to combat poverty and promote development."[9]

The Modern Popes on Poverty

This final section offers a brief glimpse at how there has been a simultaneously steady and complementary approach across the pontificates of modern popes when it comes to combating poverty. In 1961, Pope Saint John XXIII issued his encyclical *Mater et Magistra: On Christianity and Social Progress*, in which he calls on the church to consider the "temporal and eternal"[10] in service-oriented initiatives. In 1965, the Second Vatican Council gave us *Gaudium et Spes*, which places the matter of poverty in perspective yet again: "Never has the human race enjoyed such an abundance of wealth, resources, and economic power, and yet a huge proportion of the world's citizens are still tormented by hunger and poverty...."[11] In 1967, Blessed Paul VI gave us his encyclical *Populorum Progressio: On the Development of Peoples*, reminding us of the need to serve those in material poverty while remedying "the moral poverty of

---

8. John Paul II, *Ecclesia in Asia*, 7.
9. John Paul II, *Ecclesia in America*, 62.
10. John XXIII, *Mater et Magistra*, 3–5.
11. Paul VI, *Gaudium et Spes*, 4.

those who are crushed under the weight of their self-love."[12] You have already seen some examples of Saint John Paul II's calls to more effectively alleviate the plight of those living in degrading poverty. Benedict XVI echoes Paul VI's assessment by reminding us of the perils of both material and spiritual poverty, including in his 2005 encyclical *Deus Caritas Est*: "Despite the great advances made in science and technology, each day we see how much suffering there is in the world on account of different kinds of poverty, both material and spiritual."[13]

In the present day, the contributions of Pope Francis to combating global poverty can hardly be exaggerated. Pope Francis has called on everyone of good will to serve those who are marginalized in our midst. Well before he became pope, he embraced an interpersonal approach to serving those in poverty, as we see in this excerpt from *On Heaven and Earth*, which while serving as archbishop of Buenos Aires he coauthored with his friend Rabbi Abraham Skorka: "In Christianity, the attitude that we must have toward the poor is, in its essence, that of true commitment,"[14] further stressing that, "this commitment must be person to person, in the flesh. It is not enough to mediate this commitment through institutions...."[15]

Looking to the bishops as an example, the faithful should continue to seek ways to serve the downtrodden. One way is to become familiar with the Pontifical Council for Justice and Peace's 2005 *Compendium of the Social Doctrine of the Church*, which offers us the following crucial reminder: "Human activity, when it aims at promoting the integral dignity and vocation of the person, the quality of living conditions, and the meeting in solidarity of peoples and nations, is in accordance with the plan of God, who does not fail to show his love and providence to his children."[16]

12. Paul VI, *Populorum Progressio*, 21.
13. Benedict XVI, *Deus Caritas Est*, 30a.
14. Bergoglio and Skorka, *On Heaven and Earth*, 168.
15. Ibid.
16. Pontifical Council for Justice and Peace, *Compendium of the Social Doctrine of the Church*, 35.

Ultimately, serving our fellow man brings increasingly greater glory to the very figure who showed us what it means to share in the poverty of others: the Lord Jesus Christ, who has come "to bring glad tidings to the poor" (Luke 4:18).

13

The Public Square and the Church
Complementing, Not Excluding

"But Peter and the apostles said in reply, 'We must obey God rather than men.'"

(ACTS 5:29)

Is it possible to live as a faithful Catholic and a faithful citizen? Few questions could be as conditional as such a quip, especially before considering the type of government in which the aspirant person of faith is living. Over the course of the last nearly two millennia, some societal structures have facilitated the possibility of living one's Catholic faith openly, without fear of reprisals or suppression, let alone outright oppression. However, there has never been an "easy" time to strive for sainthood within the midst of *any* culture. For example, let us recall that even in the midst of the Spanish Inquisition (the *cause célèbre* of those who have claimed that the church—especially during Christendom—was a theocratic instrument bent on forcing her will on the faithful and unfaithful alike), some of the most renowned figures who are now canonized saints, such as Teresa of Ávila and John of the Cross, fell out of the favor of those ecclesial authorities who had lost sight of the purportedly sanctifying scope of their pastoral duties.

Now, well into the twenty-first century, in much of the West in particular, striving to live faithfully can be challenging, but this is due more and more to rampant secularism, as manifestations of faith result in sideways glances at best or speculations of subdued lunacy at worst. Yet, in order to remain objective in this regard, references to the church in the public square tend to have to do more with institutional religious initiatives within the broader midst of governmental oversight than with individual exercises of faith, although the two are not mutually exclusive by any regard, as particular cases have brought to light. The following are some ways in which our bishops have continuously and faithfully served their flock, often—but, of course, not always—in the midst of antagonistic governmental responses. As such, interactions between church (emphasis on the lowercase "c") and state need not be inherently adversarial, but should reflect an ongoing dialogue to establish policies that benefit all, especially the most innocent, from the defenseless unborn child to the disregarded elderly and infirm. A key emphasis of this chapter will be on how the church, with faithful bishops at the helm, has positively served society, and continues to do so, come what may, offering a complementary approach to service that infuses considerations of faith into multiple avenues of public frameworks of society.

God's Authority and Legitimate Human Authority

Following the tumult that constituted much of the twentieth century, the word *authority* earned a certain sting in the West. For example, on either side of the ideological spectrum, the malignantly supposed "authority" of the Nazis under Hitler and of the Soviets under Stalin resulted in the annihilation of countless human lives. Unfortunately, the idea of authority itself became suspect, to the exclusion of affording due regard to the acknowledgment of *legitimate* authority. As such, the Christian must recognize legitimate human authority, as do those of most other mainstream faiths.

Further addressing God's authority and legitimate human authority, when it comes to fathoming the occasionally tenuous dynamic between God's law and man's law, which sometimes intersect (particularly when they are borne of legitimate human authority), but sometimes do not, it is important to strive to strike that critical balance between giving "Caesar" and God what is due to them (see Matt 22:15-22). Archbishop Chaput, in his 2008 book, *Render unto Caesar: Serving the Nation by Living Our Catholic Beliefs in Political Life*, whose title is from Matt 22:15-22 (cf. Mark 12:13-77 and Luke 20:20-26), gives the following consideration regarding the challenge that this entails: "It can be hard work. No detailed map exists because while human nature doesn't change, human circumstances change all the time."[1]

Changing human circumstances that do not factor in the ultimate trajectory of human nature and the natural law have led to inopportune conflicts between the government and the church throughout history. This is a reality that the bishops have had to confront in an increasingly secularized world. Looking at the situation of the United States in particular, we see that while some may assert that laws sweepingly conceived are intended to reflect the will of society—believing that otherwise morally nebulous legislation is justifiable when it reflects the prominent mindset of the populace—this may in some scenarios have claims of ethical veracity. However, when we go beneath the veneer of influential cultural overlays that so often strive to dictate precedent, we better understand the polemics that accompany this outlook.

Coincident to the church's quest for truth, which is hopefully shared by governmental institutions or those in other positions of official power, one would do well to reflect on the implications of this now-famous reminder from Saint Pope John Paul II: "Following Christ, the Church seeks the truth, which is not always the same as the majority opinion. She listens to conscience and not to power, and in this way she defends the poor and the downtrodden."[2] One governmental institution to consider is the United States Su-

---

1. Chaput, *Render unto Caesar*, 204.
2. John Paul II, *Familiaris Consortio*, 5.

preme Court. While many Supreme Court decisions throughout history have been laudable, it would be intellectually insincere to pretend that this human institution has served as a de facto authorial source of morality. After all, at various points within the history of the relatively young United States, the Supreme Court has considered "settled law" its defense of slavery (Dred Scott v. Sandford—1857), its denial of women's right to vote (Minor v. Happersett—1875), its reinforcement of racial segregation (Plessy v. Ferguson—1896), and other human rights violations. In light of these laws gone wrong, it is neither autocratic nor authoritarian, let alone theocratic, to aver that morality fashioned and deliberated by governmental enterprise is a rhetorically decrepit position; rather, it is reasonable to deduce that enduring moral truths have a divine origin: God. Who could look at the Ten Commandments and place into question the merits of their demands on humanity? Their particular interpretation is the task of objective moral theologians, yet, the goal here is not so much to delve into the fine tuning of moral theology per se; rather, this is an exposition of how the bishops have offered guidance and leadership in this regard.

Thus, the bishops have endeavored to lead the church in the midst of the public square, taking into account those altered human circumstances just described. This is most evident in terms of the various statements that bishops have offered regarding engagement on issues, yet while steering clear of formally endorsing a politician or political party. Of course, if a governmental framework is seen to be devoid of any moral defensibility, the bishops have raised the alarm to the international community. Examples include Pope Pius XI, who issued his 1931 encyclical *Non Abbiamo Bisogno: On Catholic Action in Italy* against fascism, his 1937 encyclical *Mit Brennender Sorge: On the Church and the German Reich* against Nazism, and in the same year, his encyclical *Divini Redemptoris: On Atheistic Communism*. Indeed, it is both possible and advisable for the bishops to continue to work within democracy-imbued governmental structures in order to confront the forces of totalitarianism within any realm of the ideological spectrum.

Lay Participation in the Public Square Following Vatican II

In *Render unto Caesar*, Archbishop Chaput highlights how bishops' statements have served to provide "good guidance to the faithful on issues ranging from economic justice to immigration reform,"[3] while likewise asserting that the church does not offer any "special claim to policy competence. Her task is offering basic principles for her people to apply in daily life."[4] Chaput goes on to offer the crucial distinction that, "the Catholic Church cannot stay, has never stayed, and *never will* stay 'out of politics.' Politics involves the exercise of power. The use of power has moral content and human consequences."[5] One could not, with ease, speculate that the Catholic Church should have remained out of politics when bishops got behind the U.S. Civil Rights Movement of the 1950s and 1960s, spearheaded by Rev. Dr. Martin Luther King Jr., with Archbishop (later Cardinal) Patrick O'Boyle of Washington delivering the invocation at the beginning of the August 28, 1963, March on Washington that featured King's iconic "I Have a Dream" speech.[6] A later archbishop of Washington, Cardinal Wuerl, has noted that in terms of the Christian witness expected of us regarding opposing injustices: "This principled stand has been a tremendous benefit to this country where we spend our earthly lives. We speak against inequity and oppression. We stand for human rights, especially the most fundamental right: the right to life."[7] There is no doubt that the right to life, from the unborn child, to the inmate on death row, to the severely infirm, remains a key focus of the church's promotion of civil rights extending into the twenty-first century.

The laity is called to actively participate in the political process, and to bring faith into the public sphere. This has been a steady feature of the post-Vatican II epoch. The Second Vatican

---

3. Chaput, *Render unto Caesar*, 209.
4. Ibid.
5. Ibid., 217–18.
6. Zimmermann, "A Prayer, and a Life, for Justice," August 14, 2013.
7. Wuerl, *Seek First the Kingdom*, 45.

Council happened to take place during the same era as the United States had its first Catholic president, John F. Kennedy, whose life was tragically taken by an assassin's gunfire in Texas as Catholic bishops were in the midst of actively laboring on the other side of the Atlantic for a more peaceful world. While the legacy of the Second Vatican Council, in and of itself, is met with mixed reactions among Catholics of varying perspectives, the faithful can securely affirm that it featured an array of substantive benefits. After all, the popes who called it and concluded it—John XIII and Paul VI, respectively—are now Saint John XXIII and Blessed Paul VI. In his 2016 book, *Hope for the World: To Unite All Things in Christ*, Cardinal Raymond Burke indicates the following regarding his perceptions of the Council: "I considered the Council as an extraordinary way of sharing the great richness of the life and practice of the Church,"[8] although "a certain sense of disorientation came to light."[9] Unfortunately, "people developed a sense that many aspects of the faith and of religious practice were now debatable and subject to private judgment,"[10] and "an erroneous notion of conscience developed, with disastrous effects in the moral life of Catholics."[11] In *Render unto Caesar*, Archbishop Chaput makes a similar observation:

> Vatican II assumed that Catholic citizens would serve the common good by rooting their actions in a well-formed, comprehensive, mature Catholic sense of social justice. In the United States, this has failed for various reasons. As we've already seen, American Catholic laypeople have earned great economic and educational success. They often serve the public with great skill. But their grasp of their own Catholic faith is often poor or is shaped by an unfriendly wider culture. In the way they *apply* their faith, too many American Catholics ignore what they claim—as Catholics—to believe as true."[12]

8. Burke, *Hope for the World*, 27.

9. Ibid.

10. Ibid., 28.

11. Ibid.

12. Chaput, *Render unto Caesar*, 207–208.

From a Catholic perspective, the church in the public square following the Second Vatican Council continues to face various challenges, and it is more important than ever to heed the bishops as they strive to defend and promote the role of faith in the public sector. Of course, the bishops cannot do this alone, because they are not necessarily as "in the world" as rank and file Catholics are. The bishops and the laity must cooperate when it comes to introducing faith and morality into daily life, especially including public life, because this is our shared call as those who are baptized, as Cardinal Tagle of the Archdiocese of Manila alludes to in his 2015 book, *Telling the Story of Jesus: Word—Communion—Mission*: "It is evident that the living sacrifice of the baptized includes ethical demands."[13] This is manifested when we underscore the positive aspects of the church in the public sphere, because without true charity, secular mindsets can lead to mere activism, rather than actual social justice. Hence, with the inherent intersection of the church's social teachings and the exercise of true justice, we thus heed the words of Bishop Kevin Rhoades of the Diocese of Fort Wayne in South Bend, Indiana, from his homily "Voting from a Catholic Perspective" of October 26, 2016: "The Church's social teaching should inform our consciences to recognize and fulfill the obligations of justice and charity in society. This social doctrine implies responsibilities in society, including political obligations. We are called to put the Church's social teaching into action."[14]

Religious Freedom, Clarity, and Catholic Politicians in the Public Square

Well into the twenty-first century, the Catholic Church has faced threats to religious liberty in all parts of the world. In terms of democratic governmental structures, the church has not been immune from being hauled into the courts by civil authorities for not yielding to the unjust demands of the state, perhaps most infamously in

---

13. Tagle, *Telling the Story of Jesus*, 42.
14. Rhoades, "Voting from a Catholic Perspective," 8.

the cause of the Little Sisters of the Poor in the United States, who contested being forced by the United States government to offer insurance plans that covered practices that were objectionable according to their faith. In 2016, the USCCB's Ad Hoc Committee for Religious Liberty indicated: "The Little Sisters have argued that religious freedom exists not only for houses of worship but also for those who serve others, such as in ministry to the poor, which is part and parcel of the Catholic faith."[15] Similar situations have arisen, and others may arise, but the laity can rely on the bishops to continue to offer a clear and courageous defense of religious liberty in the public square. The relations between the bishops and Catholic politicians has an occasionally curious dynamic, particularly as far as the *sensus fidei* is concerned, and prelates such as Cardinal Francis George have reminded the laity of the irreplaceable role of bishops: "We speak for the apostolic faith, and those who hold it gather round. We must listen to the sensus fidei . . . but this is different from intellectual trends and public opinion."[16]

A conclusion that mentions the dynamic between the bishops and Catholic politicians is due. Catholic political figures are typically the most powerful lay Catholics in society. As such, their example is rather prominent. Unfortunately, some Catholic faithful may be more drawn to heed the advice of dissident Catholic politicians than the wisdom of their bishops. Myriad examples could be offered of times when Catholic bishops have patiently and charitably called on Catholic politicians to review the church's teachings on topics from the sanctity of human life, to immigration, to the uniqueness of marriage, and so on. Documents such as the USCCB's *Forming Consciences for Faithful Citizenship* have offered guidance to both voter and candidate.

Although much of the focus of this chapter has been on the American political system, the global scope of what this entails has likewise been addressed in such writings as then-Cardinal Ratzinger's 2002 aptly named document, *Doctrinal Note on Some*

15. United States Conference of Catholic Bishops, *Witnesses to Freedom*, 1.

16. *America*, "Health Care Disunity Revisited in George's USCCB Address," November 15, 2010.

Questions Regarding the Participation of Catholics in Political Life. It is advisable for Catholics in all walks of life to read this short document in order to better comprehend the challenging role for which Catholic politicians are accountable. With the common good of society—including that which is ideally furthered in the public square by way of the government—as the shared goal of not only the baptized, but of all citizens of good will, Catholic politicians and Catholics in all walks of life would be wise to heed Cardinal Wuerl's prudent and seasoned counsel: "The pastors of the church, the pope, and bishops, have been explicitly charged to guide the faithful in the way of salvation. They are the fixed point in a changing world. Since they are accountable to sacred tradition, they represent objectivity against the subjective claims of the individual."[17]

---

17. Wuerl, *Seek First the Kingdom*, 104.

14

Racial and Ethnic Harmony
Restoring and Promoting Societal Accord

"God created mankind in his image;
in the image of God he created them."
(GEN 1:27A)

Prior to entering into any coverage of the challenges presented by racism, it is necessary to first emphasize that everyone is made in God's *image* and *likeness* (see Gen 1:26–27). You may recall that the chapter on international relations was headed by that iconic passage from Galatians: "for you are all one in Christ Jesus" (3:28b). Let us take a moment to consider the beginning part of that passage: "There is neither Jew nor Greek, there is neither slave nor free person, there is not male and female" (Gal 3:28a). The Apostle Paul's point is not that two different people have no distinguishing characteristics between them; rather, we all share equal worth, value, and dignity as humans. Although the term "equality" has taken on a breadth of frequently charged and variant meanings in modern parlance, the Christian message ushers in a certain *equality* in accordance with our common brotherhood reflective of God's goodness.

Racial and Ethnic Harmony

Bishops from around the world, from those of local dioceses to the pope, have discussed the matter of racism from a variety of angles, particularly over the course of the last one hundred years. Prior to entering into the bishops' assessments, diagnoses, and ultimate Christian response to racial discord, it is worthwhile to embark on an cursory overview of the history of the Catholic Church and the dynamics of race. On that note, it is critical to remember that in modern English, we speak often of *race*, when we are really referring to the more accurate term of *ethnicity*. Nonetheless, since this chapter does not feature a treatise on linguistics, in order to make recourse to mainstream terminology, we will use the term *race* more prominently than *ethnicity*.

Church History and the Dynamics of Race

Let us look, of course, first and foremost to the Gospels. The biblical exegete will immediately assert that there is no description of Jesus' physical characteristics in any segment of the New Testament. We are aware that Jesus was a male, an Israelite (a Galilean, to be more precise), and that he died when he was approximately thirty-three years old. Over the course of the last nearly two millennia, visual artists, authors, and other shapers of culture have delivered renditions of Jesus featuring practically every possible skin pigment, eye color, hair texture, height, body composition, and other physiological categorization. It is probably beneficial that the Gospel writers offered no indication of what Jesus looked like, because that serves as a reminder that God incarnated himself in order to offer his gift of salvation to humanity, no matter our particular ethnic background. Recall again, from the chapter on international relations, how the Apostle Philip brought the message of Jesus Christ as far as Ethiopia (see Acts 8:26–40).

The point must be made initially and poignantly that, unfortunately, during the last two thousand years, some Catholics, while bearing the banner of the Lord Jesus Christ, have defiled the reputation of the church by committing acts fueled by racism. During the Age of Exploration and European colonization, too many "Catholic" explorers, conquistadors, and national sovereigns sought *glory* and *gold* rather than God, deeming many indigenous people and those of African descent as racially inferior in order to dehumanize and therefore control them, effectively disregarding God and his expectations regarding charity, mercy, and compassion. They did this under the mantle of the church. While slavery was an institution in the United States, some bishops and other priests even had slaves. Meanwhile, some clergymen condoned segregation based on race in southern schools. Fortunately, in the ambiance of this caustic racial disharmony, righteous and saintly figures arose, many of whom have been canonized. One need simply think of the contributions of Bartolomé de las Casas (1484–1566), Saint Martín de Porres (1579–1639), Saint Peter Claver (1581–1654), Saint Katharine Drexel (1858–1955), and various others who actively worked for harmony and reconciliation between people of different races by speaking out against the animosity and unjust power structures in place during their times.

The Catholic Church had already been established for nearly 1,500 years (see Matt 16:18) before it had to confront race relations as we understand them today. Prior to this, interactions between different groups typically came in the form of dialoguing with those of varying religious faiths, national affiliations, cultural traditions, languages, and so forth. Perceiving one another as having different worth based on nothing more than skin color was a disturbing social construct that gained increasing traction around the 1500s.

Since we have already conceded that some bearing the banner of the church unfortunately used their positions of social influence to commit atrocious acts based on racism, we can look at what took place in the midst of the Age of Exploration regarding the church's reassertion of Christ's teachings. Regarding evangelization on a large scale (see the chapter on evangelization), multiple forces within the church came to acknowledge that spreading the Good News never means eradicating someone's identity, whether in terms of his or her ethnic background, culture, or any intersection thereof. As such, it is possible to maintain fidelity to the Gospel while recognizing the contributions of those of different ethnic classifications, linguistic families, or other distinct cultural characteristics.

Having established this understanding of what has transpired during church history regarding race relations, over the last five hundred years in particular, comparing those who worked for the Gospel and those who did not always adhere to it, we can now transition into looking at the official teachings of the church, as passed down by the popes through the centuries. These teachings either directly or indirectly opposed racism and its ill effects, and afforded dignity to those of all ethnic backgrounds.

Over the last approximately five hundred years, multiple popes, functioning as vicars of Christ, have acted according to the Magisterium by writing statements in condemnation of the institution of slavery, as well as other human rights abuses. In 1435, Pope Eugene IV wrote *Sicut Dudum* in opposition to the enslavement of Africans in the Canary Islands (Spain); the next century, in 1537, Paul III issued his *Sublimus Dei* against the enslavement of the indigenous peoples in the Americas, while still promoting their evangelization as fellow children of the Almighty; in 1839, Gregory XVI wrote his apostolic letter *In Supremo Apostolatus*, further condemning the slave trade; in 1888, Leo XIII's encyclical *In Plurimis* advocated the abolition of slavery, and only two years later, in 1890, Leo's encyclical *Catholicae Ecclesiae* spoke out against the practice of slavery in the church's mission territories. To be frank, some within the church defied the church's clear teachings, thereby defying the Gospel in the process, by not heeding the church's emphasis on the inherent dignity of every single person.

This section has merely served as a brief overview of the sequence of race relations within the Catholic Church. It was hardly exhaustive, but has hopefully served to provide a glimpse at what has occurred that is of note. This brings us to the efforts that the bishops have undertaken to address racial inequalities, prejudice, and other manifestations of racism that have evidenced themselves since the twentieth century in particular.

Bishops and Particular Racial Situations in the United States

You will recall that, during the Age of Exploration, the Catholic Church undertook efforts at evangelization around the globe that led to a greater embrace of the diverse ethnic tapestry that ultimately reflects the kingdom of God. Yet, what takes place when those of any religious affiliation do not respect the rich beauty of ethnic diversity? Let us look to Cardinal Wuerl for a dose of prudent advice, from his book *The Catholic Way*:

> What should be a blessing—the diversity of our backgrounds, experiences, and cultures—becomes a hindrance to unity and a heavy burden for some to bear. As we struggle to remove the attitudes that nurture racism and the actions that express it, we must show how the differences we find in skin color, national origin, or cultural diversity are enriching.[1]

In tandem with Cardinal Wuerl's perspective, other American Catholic bishops have offered writings over the last few decades that directly address the church's approach to race relations. A crucial feature of these ecclesial texts is that, unlike too many (although, of course, not all) political pundits or prominent personalities who have fomented anger, dissention, and bitterness rather than actual good will, the bishops have instead provided the church's charitable outlook, which is reflective of the Gospel, and thereby geared toward the true harmony, reconciliation, and peace that originates with Christ alone (see John 14:27).

Take, for instance, the following reminders from the United States Conference of Catholic Bishops' 1979 pastoral letter, *Brothers and Sisters to Us*: "Indeed, racism is more than a disregard for the words of Jesus; it is a denial of the truth of the dignity of each human being revealed by the mystery of the Incarnation. In order to find the strength to overcome the evil of racism, we must look to Christ,"[2] and "the Christian response to the challenges of our times

---

1. Wuerl, *The Catholic Way*, 322.
2. United States Conference of Catholic Bishops, *Brothers and Sisters to*

is to be found in the Good News of Jesus."[3] To continue along this line of thought, another point that merits significant consideration insofar as responding to the injustice of racism is necessarily framed within the greater context of our imitation of Christ: "The ultimate remedy against evils such as this will not come solely from human effort. What is needed is the recreation of the human being according to the image revealed in Jesus Christ. For he reveals in himself what each human being can and must become."[4] Likewise, in this passage, we find the very point that provides us with the title for the text:

> Therefore, let the Church proclaim to all that the sin of racism defiles the image of God and degrades the sacred dignity of humankind which has been revealed by the mystery of the Incarnation. Let all know that it is a terrible sin that mocks the cross of Christ and ridicules the Incarnation. For the brother and sister of our Brother Jesus Christ are brother and sister to us.[5]

It is with good reason that *Brothers and Sisters to Us* has served as such a formative text that it continues to be referenced within discussions of race relations well into the twenty-first century. Subsequently, there are other writings from the bishops that are indicative of the leadership role that the church has embraced in facilitating discussions on how to realize racial accord at this juncture in history, perhaps particularly in the United States. A few such examples follow.

In 1984, the black bishops of the United States issued *'What We Have Seen and Heard': A Pastoral Letter on Evangelization from the Black Bishops of the United States*. Given its broader scope, *'What We Have Seen and Heard'* does not focus directly on the dilemma of racism per se; rather, it invites us to once again view the merits of the rich ethnic tapestry that constitutes the church. Furthermore, *'What We Have Seen and Heard'* promotes harmony

---

Us, 3.

3. Ibid., 7.
4. Ibid., 8–9.
5. Ibid., 10.

and reconciliation between those of different backgrounds, such as in this excerpt that identifies the unity of mission in service to the Gospel throughout the church:

> [W]e must at the beginning remember those who brought us to new birth within the faith. When we as black Catholics speak of missionaries, we shall never forget the devoted service that many white priests, vowed religious, and laypersons gave to us as a people and still give to us daily. We shall remember and never forget that this ministry was often given at great personal sacrifice and hardship. The same holds true today.[6]

On that note, it is of little surprise that in subsequent years, including at the turn of the twenty-first century, when the bishops looked to the new millennium with hope, bishops of varied ethnic backgrounds issued numerous writings in order to foster reconciliation and to teach why racism is such a pernicious injustice. In June of 2000, the United States Conference of Catholic Bishops published an extensive collection of statements made by American bishops, particularly between 1997 and June 2000. This compilation, titled, *Love Thy Neighbor as Thyself: U.S. Catholic Bishops Speak Against Racism*, was organized by the USCCB's Committee on African-American Catholics (which is now called the Subcommittee on African-American Affairs). In the preface, Bishop George Murry, SJ, calls on us to "lead by example in eliminating this sin that divides the human family."[7]

The Twenty-First Century, Globalism, and Aspirations for Accord

In the twenty-first century, bishops have continued to write against the dilemma of racism, and have offered exceptionally pastoral suggestions regarding how to restore peace and justice. In 2003, Bishop

---

6. United States Conference of Catholic Bishops, *'What We Have Seen and Heard,'* 3.

7. United States Conference of Catholic Bishops, *Love Thy Neighbor as Thyself*, 1.

Dale Melczek of Gary, Indiana, wrote *Created in God's Image: A Pastoral Letter on the Sin of Racism and a Call to Conversion*, in which he reminds us of what the church continues to profess: "We truly are all members of the same human family, and each of us is sacred by virtue of the fact that we are a reflection of our God. This is a fundamental religious truth and the grounds for respecting all human life."[8] On January 1, 2015, Bishop Edward Braxton of Belleville, Illinois, wrote *The Racial Divide in the United States: A Reflection for the World Day of Peace* 2015. Bishop Braxton closes his reflection with these words that lead us to reflect on the implications of how God took on human flesh in the form of Jesus Christ, participating in humanity in the interest of everyone in the process:

> That saving birth confronts and comforts each of us with the life-giving, sin-shattering truth. Before God there is no racial divide because the life, teachings, wondrous signs, suffering, death, resurrection, and ascension of Christ and his Pentecost gift of the Holy Spirit has redeemed us all.[9]

Let us remember that, returning to the overview of church history vis-à-vis race relations that we briefly examined, from a historical perspective, racism is a relatively new phenomenon in human history. The bishops, in collaboration with organizations such as the National Black Catholic Congress, the USCCB's Secretariat of Cultural Diversity in the Church (which includes the Subcommittee on African-American Affairs recently referenced), and other groups, will continue to offer charitable voices of enduring reconciliation. May they continue to lead us to celebrate the church's remarkable ethnic tapestry, bringing greater glory to the Creator of us all.

---

8. Melczek, *Created in God's Image*, 9.
9. Braxton, *The Racial Divide in the United States*, 17.

15

Sanctity of Human Life
Celebrating the First and Ultimate of All Rights

"I call heaven and earth today to witness against you: I have set before you life and death, the blessing and the curse. Choose life, then, that you and your descendants may live, by loving the Lord, your God, obeying his voice, and holding fast to him."
(DEUT 30:19–20)

Few topics are as controversial as those which the church collectively regards as the "right to life." Abortion. Embryonic stem cell research. Capital punishment. Unjust war. Euthanasia and physician-assisted suicide. The Catholic Church is opposed to these and other such practices that literally deaden societies. However, the church is not simply "against" these practices; rather, it is truly *pro-life* in easily the most accurate sense of the term.

The twentieth century was easily the deadliest in human history, and the twenty-first century appears poised to rival that designation. It is not mere opinion or conjecture to venture to ascertain that, despite the "advancements" that global societies have undertaken in the centuries that have comprised the wake of the Enlightenment, threats to human life are more widely varied and nefarious than ever before. The bishops around the world have come out in force to restore a "Culture of Life" in the interest of humanity broadly. Fortunately, there are far more examples of their writings on pro-life efforts than can be listed or described in one chapter, or even in one book, for that matter. The following sections detail what has taken place over the course of the last few decades in particular, as well as bishops' evaluations regarding how the church can bring about a global culture that draws humanity to recall that life is God's greatest gift of all.

The Continued Aftermath of the Sexual Revolution

In the chapter on human sexuality, you saw how bishops have attempted to help their flocks recover from the effects of the Sexual Revolution. While it may seem inopportune to return to this matter here, it is necessary to first consider the link that the church maintains between chastity and the Culture of Life, and what occurs when society begins to reject chastity on a wider scale. A prime example is the increase in abortions that has taken place within the last few decades, with the United States serving as a notorious example.

Thus, looking to the bishops in the United States, it is worthwhile to first visit the destructive effect that the Sexual Revolution continues to have on society on a global scale. Let us look, for example, at the words of Cardinal Timothy Dolan of New York, who, in speaking about his brother bishops in Africa in the midst of the Extraordinary Synod of Bishops on the Family in October of 2014, offered the following assessment of how the bishops around the world can support each other in terms of reminding themselves to stay the course in the midst of worldly concerns:

> We in the Church in Europe, the Church in North America, we suffer sometimes from a lethargy, don't we? Not Africa! . . . The bishops of Africa are prophetic in reminding us that the role of the Church is to transform the culture, not to be transformed by the culture . . . I'm

afraid sometimes we in the West might say, "Oh, I guess we ought to dilute things, I guess we ought to capitulate, it's obvious this teaching's being rejected, oh my Lord, we're not popular." And the Africans say, "Well, you know what? We're not supposed to be. What we're supposed to do is propose the truth and invite people by the love and the joy of our lives to embrace the truth. And take it from us, brothers, it works."[1]

Cardinal Dolan's words ring true in terms of how faithful bishops have not given in when it comes to professing how fidelity to Christ's teachings rests at the core of any considerations of the multiple dimensions of the Culture of Life. Despite the temporal power and pervasive influence of the Sexual Revolution, and the barrage of deviant messages that the movement has furthered, courageous bishops have kept in heart and mind Saint Paul's words: "Do not conform yourself to this age, but be transformed by the renewal of your mind, that you may discern what is the will of God, what is good and pleasing and perfect" (Rom 12:2). In an epoch in which the outcomes of the Sexual Revolution are evidenced more and more every day, the bishops can embrace the fortitude that their pastoral role entails and demands, in order to lead the faithful to a more profound understanding of what constitutes the Culture of Life.

Transitioning into a discussion of how the church celebrates all human life leads us from looking at the setting of the Sexual Revolution to a wider comprehension of how the twenty-first century world has presented an entirely new set of challenges that were not in place in prior generations. This is especially lamentable in light of the technological innovations that have taken place in the modern era—many of which have benefited humanity, but others of which have introduced new categories of destructiveness that threaten broad swaths of humanity, from the unborn child to the elderly infirm to the innocent civilian during wartime. As such, it is crucial to look at what the church recognizes: the divinely-originated inviolability, dignity, and value of all human life, in all its forms and stages.

1. *Catholic World Report*, "Cardinals Kasper and Dolan and the African Bishops," October 15, 2014.

The Bishops and Valuing Life in All Its Stages

In Pope Saint John Paul II's book, *Love and Responsibility*, originally published in 1960 when he was an auxiliary bishop of Krakow, he reminds us "that morally, termination of pregnancy is a very grave offense."[2] Blessed Paul VI's *Humanae Vitae*, which has been mentioned, discusses abortion and sterilization as pernicious affronts to God's plan for chastity and marriage, and thus stresses the church's interest in respecting human life:

> Therefore we base our words on the first principles of a human and Christian doctrine of marriage when we are obliged once more to declare that the direct interruption of the generative process already begun and, above all, all direct abortion, even for therapeutic reasons, are to be absolutely excluded as lawful means of regulating the number of children. Equally to be condemned, as the Magisterium of the Church has affirmed on many occasions, is direct sterilization, whether of the man or of the woman, whether permanent or temporary.[3]

Abortion deserves a concerted degree of preoccupation due to its sheer magnitude, with millions of unborn lives being lost each year around the globe. The enormity of abortion as a global human rights nightmare sends shudders through the properly formed conscience.

In the mid-1990s, as the West continued to see the continued onslaught of abortion, John Paul II issued his watershed encyclical *Evangelium Vitae: On the Value and Inviolability of Human Life*. In *Evangelium Vitae*, John Paul II discusses both how and why the church is opposed to threats against human life throughout the spectrum, thus speaking out against abortion, the destruction of embryos, capital punishment, murder, genocide, the instigation of armed conflicts, and any other threat to the "sacred value of human life from its very beginning until its end,"[4] since we "can affirm the right of every human being to have this primary good respected

---

2. John Paul II, *Love and Responsibility*, 285.
3. Paul VI, *Humanae Vitae*, 14.
4. John Paul II, *Evangelium Vitae*, 2.

to the highest degree."⁵ Note the particular forcefulness of Saint John Paul II's words against abortion specifically: "Among all the crimes which can be committed against life, procured abortion has characteristics making it particularly serious and deplorable."⁶

Yet, is the Catholic Church merely "pro-birth," and not truly "pro-life," as some both within and outside of the church have posited? Does the church focus too much attention on the opposition to abortion, to the exclusion of not recognizing the need to protect and support people in other stages of development across all realms of society? It turns out that, no, this argument holds little water, as Archbishop Chaput of Philadelphia has reinforced with the following prescient assessment regarding how the church indeed defends life in all its manifold stages and individual situations. Note how Archbishop Chaput references Cardinal Joseph Bernardin's now-famous allusion to the *seamless garment of life* that is reflective of a consistent life ethic that underpins the church's embrace of life from the very moment of conception until our natural demise, as well as the United States Conference of Catholic Bishops' document *Living the Gospel of Life*, which we will address imminently. First, according to Chaput:

> The deliberate killing of innocent life is a uniquely wicked act. No amount of contextualizing or deflecting our attention to other issues can obscure that. This is precisely why Cardinal John O'Connor, Bishop James McHugh, and others pressed so hard for the passage of the U.S. bishops' 1998 pastoral letter, *Living the Gospel of Life*. As Cardinal Joseph Bernardin once wisely noted, Catholic social teaching is a seamless garment of respect for human life, from conception to natural death. It makes no sense to champion the cause of unborn children if we ignore their basic needs once they're born. Thus it's no surprise that—year in and year out—nearly all Catholic dioceses in the United States, including Philadelphia, devote far more time, personnel, and material resources

5. Ibid.
6. Ibid., 58.

The Bishops' Efforts to Restore a More Enduring Culture of Life

As Archbishop Chaput has made reference to, the United States Conference of Catholic Bishops issued their statement *Living the Gospel of Life: A Challenge to American Catholics—A Statement by the Catholic Bishops of the United States* in 1998. This document came only a few years after John Paul II's *Evangelium Vitae* (1995). Within the opening lines of *Living the Gospel of Life*, we see the bishops of the United States taking seriously their pastoral role in the interest of fostering guiding principles to the American laity, leading them closer to the Lord and his charity-laden teachings: "In this statement we attempt to fulfill our role as teachers and pastors in proclaiming the Gospel of Life. We are confident that the proclamation of the truth in love is an indispensible way for us to exercise our pastoral responsibility."[8]

Although focusing on the scourge of abortion in particular, due to the gravity of the situation as far as its large-scale threat to innocent human life in its most vulnerable form, *Living the Gospel of Life* also calls on everyone of good will to understand the church's consistent ethic of life, insofar as other menaces to the Culture of Life are concerned:

> Opposition to abortion and euthanasia does not excuse indifference to those who suffer from poverty, violence, and injustice. Any politics of human life must work to resist the violence of war and the scandal of capital punishment. Any politics of human dignity must seriously address issues of racism, poverty, hunger, employment, education, housing, and health care. Therefore, Catholics

---

7. Chaput, "There Is No Equivalence," August 10, 2015.

8. United States Conference of Catholic Bishops, *Living the Gospel of Life*, Introduction.

should eagerly involve themselves as advocates for the weak and marginalized in all these areas.[9]

The church holds these *weak* and *marginalized* in various regards, and one of these populations is life in its embryonic stages:

> The issue of stem cell research does not force us to choose between science and ethics, much less between science and religion. It presents a choice as to how our society will pursue scientific and medical progress. Will we ignore ethical norms and use some of the most vulnerable human beings as objects, undermining the respect for human life that is at the foundation of the healing arts?[10]

As we have seen, since the inception of the Sexual Revolution in the 1960s, the Catholic Church's teachings on chastity and the dignity of all human life remain at odds with various categories of popular sentiment. Nonetheless, the bishops have continuously focused attention on why the church is pro-life: because God is the origin of all human life, and because we are made in his image and likeness (see Gen 1:26–27). The bishops have maintained this outlook by continuing to proclaim the Gospel of Life, including by confronting the myriad new threats to human life presented as we continue in the twenty-first century.

The Bishops, Mercy, and Compassion in the Twenty-First Century

The Bishops have faced a new menace to the Culture of Life in the twenty-first century, in the form of physician-assisted suicide and euthanasia. Subsequently, the bishops have increasingly had to delineate and clarify what actually constitutes mercy and compassion. For example, in the United States Conference of Catholic Bishops' June 2011 document, *To Live Each Day with Dignity: A Statement on Physician-Assisted Suicide*, the bishops remind us

---

9. Ibid., 21.

10. United States Conference of Catholic Bishops, *On Embryonic Stem Cell Research*, Conclusion.

that, "the sufferings caused by chronic or terminal illness are often severe. They cry out for our compassion, a word whose root meaning is to 'suffer with' another person. True compassion alleviates suffering while maintaining solidarity with those who suffer."[11]

The bishops have likewise proclaimed that dignity remains a paramount consideration. They have done this by relying on the church's precedent that all life is worth defending. Take, for instance, how the bishops of Maryland, via the Maryland Catholic Conference, relied on the arguments that Saint John Paul II presented in *Evangelium Vitae* when they offered the following assessment regarding euthanasia in their November 2014 text, *Comfort and Consolation: Care for the Sick and Dying—A Pastoral Letter from the Catholic Bishops of Maryland*: "No matter how good the motives might seem, euthanasia is always an immoral attack on human life and a false compassion that is unable to see the abiding dignity of the human person in all conditions and circumstances."[12]

A Final Note: Human Life and the Bishops' Imitation of Jesus the Good Shepherd

The claim is often made that, "Jesus did not discuss [this topic] or [that topic] in the Gospels." If we were to make a list, it would be long indeed. We do not live in an era in which human life is valued as it should be. Pope Francis has frequently criticized the "throwaway culture" that disregards that which is deemed expendable, even including human life itself. We look to the bishops to continue modeling Jesus, as the "Good Shepherd" (see John 10:1–21), thus protecting their flock and speaking with a voice that echoes the Lord's, especially when he proclaims "I came so that they might have life and have it more abundantly" (John 10:10).

---

11. United States Conference of Catholic Bishops, *To Live Each Day with Dignity*, 4.

12. Maryland Catholic Conference, Comfort and Consolation, 8; cf. John Paul II, *Evangelium Vitae*, 64–65.

16

A Conclusive Message of Gratitude for Our Bishops

"I will appoint for you shepherds after my own heart, who will shepherd you wisely and prudently."

(JER 3:15)

Thus we conclude this cursory—and hopefully exemplary, in the more accurate sense of the term—overview of how the bishops' writings, particularly since the late nineteenth century, have contributed to drawing the laity closer to the Lord Jesus Christ. It is hoped that the laity will make recourse to more of the bishops' writings, in order to learn more, and thus fortify, their Catholic faith. Of course, there are more topics than could be adequately covered in a book of this scope, and the faithful look to the example of, and offer our gratitude to, our bishops for the leadership that they have offered in various ways, including their writings. A few examples follow.

In the midst of war and threats of violence around the globe, we look to such documents as Saint John XXIII's 1963 encyclical, *Pacem in Terris: On Establishing Universal Peace in Truth, Justice, Charity, and Liberty*, or the United States Conference of Catholic

A Conclusive Message of Gratitude for Our Bishops

Bishops' 1983 document, *The Challenge of Peace: God's Promise and Our Response—A Pastoral Letter on War and Peace*. Considering a world that attempts to drive a wedge between matters of science and faith, we have such documents as Saint John Paul II's 1998 encyclical *Fides et Ratio: On the Relationship Between Faith and Reason*. When it comes to the bishops inspiring their fellow priests, we have such titles as John Paul II's 1996 book, *Gift and Mystery: On the Fiftieth Anniversary of My Priestly Ordination*, or Archbishop José Gómez's 2009 book, *Men of Brave Heart: The Virtue of Courage in the Priestly Life*. In order to become more acquainted with the beauty of the sacramental life, centered of course on the Eucharist, we can read such writings as John Paul II's 2003 encyclical, *Ecclesia de Eucharistia: On the Eucharist and Its Relationship to the Church*. If a layperson wants to learn more about the implications of widespread use of electronic technology and social media during this Digital Age, long before the Internet became what it is today, there was the Vatican II document *Inter Mirifica: Decree on the Media of Social Communications* (1963). Numerous such examples abound of how the bishops' writings can draw the laity to a greater comprehension of how to best serve the Lord pursuant to our universal call to holiness.

Although the laity in particular was the audience of the first fifteen chapters of this book, this chapter in particular is intended principally for the bishops. (Frankly, anyone of good will is of course welcome to read any part of this book, but the goal here is to narrow the orientation toward the episcopate.) First and foremost, it should be noted that no part of this book has been intended to exclude any particular bishop(s), e.g., within the realm of the English-speaking world, because each man has his own gifts to share within his pastoral role as a prelate. However, frankly, some write more than others. Likewise, it would be impossible to mention everyone by name. Nonetheless, a collective word to our bishops: Thank you for your ministry!

It is fitting to offer within this message of gratitude an excerpt from the beginning of the 1965 Vatican II document, *Christus Dominus: Decree Concerning the Pastoral Office of Bishops*:

"Therefore, [Jesus] sanctified them, conferring on them the Holy Spirit, so that they also might glorify the Father upon earth and save men, 'to the building up of the body of Christ' (Eph 4:12), which is the Church."[1] Blessed Paul VI, who closed the Second Vatican Council, bore the name of Saint Paul, Apostle to the Gentiles, who offered a comparable charge during his farewell speech at Miletus: "Keep watch over yourselves and over the whole flock of which the Holy Spirit has appointed you overseers, in which you tend the church of God that he acquired with his own blood" (Acts 20:28). So far, so good. However, Paul continued with a stark, dire, and sobering warning: "I know that after my departure, savage wolves will come among you, and they will not spare the flock. And from your own group, men will come forward perverting the truth to draw the disciples away after them" (Acts 20:29-30). Thank you to those bishops who have so ardently defended their flock against the forces of darkness that have sought to besiege the church across millennia. Many such bishops have become saints by thus shepherding the people of God.

These are indeed challenging times for the church, whether for the clergy, professed religious, or the laity alike. We in the laity thus give thanks for our many strong and courageous bishops, leaders imbued with fortitude and patience, teaching the truth in charity and striving to lead their flock heavenward. On that note, we are occasionally tempted to think of the church in terms of "conservative" Catholics or "liberal" Catholics, but such an assessment is severely inadequate. Such merely political terminology did not even exist two thousand years ago, and it is inadequate to apply such designations—whose implications change with the breeze (observe, for example, what Republicans and Democrats furthered 150 years ago, as compared to now)—to ecclesial matters. Still, while heading the Diocese of Salt Lake City, Bishop George Niederauer offered the following consideration in his 2004 book, *Precious as Silver: Imagining Your Life with God*: "Over forty years ago a professor of mine was asked whether he favored liberals or conservatives in government. He replied 'That's like asking

---

1. Paul VI, *Christus Dominus*, 1.

whether I want an accelerator or brakes on my car."[2] As has been addressed, although the terms "liberal" and "conservative" remain demonstrably insufficient, the point still offers a worthy juxtaposition. Nonetheless, in ecclesial matters, more appropriate terms are *orthodox* and *heterodox* (again, not that either term perfectly aligns itself with the political expressions "conservative" or "liberal" [or even "moderate," let alone any other linguistic intersection thereof]). We thus give thanks for the multitude of bishops who so patiently embrace orthodoxy—"right reading," and thus inspire the laity to assent to the beautifully arrayed truths inherent to the Good News of Jesus Christ, coincident to the kingdom of God, rather than to fall into spiritual folly or confused waywardness in matters of faith and morals. We need, and are capable of heeding, real shepherds who lovingly protect their flock from wandering into the thorny fields of the toleration of moral relativism.

The church is grateful for prelates who further orthodoxy and lead in a manner reflective of Christ's teachings on both mercy and justice, calling us as laypersons to repentance and ongoing interior conversion. We are grateful for figures such as Archbishop Chaput, who in *Render unto Caesar* has offered the reminder that, "bishops do need to give clear Catholic teaching to their people."[3] We thank Cardinal Raymond Burke for drawing us to recall via *Hope for the World* that, "The circumstances in which [a bishop] carries out his God-given vocation may change, but the responsibilities that result from the grace he has received never change."[4] Cardinal Arinze offers a related reminder, this time juxtaposing the roles of the laity and the episcopate within the church, in his 2013 book *The Layperson's Distinctive Role*:

> Bishops and priests are the pastors in the Church. This is a question of sacramental designation through the Sacrament of Holy Orders. In the diocese, it is the bishop who is the leader in the Church. In particular, he is the teacher and pastor in questions of faith and morals. It is

2. Niederauer, *Precious as Silver*, 9.
3. Chaput, *Render unto Caesar*, 209.
4. Burke, *Hope for the World*, 122.

he who authoritatively teaches the people what they are to believe and what they are to do or not to do in order to attain salvation.⁵

We give thanks for bishops who lead so pastorally, in grace and truth, for their sole interest is in leading their flock on their walk with the Lord Jesus Christ, lest the faithful end up cast adrift, tossed around on the frigid and choppy seas of what the world claims is acceptable.

We are grateful for the insights of prelates such as Bishop Steven Lopes, the first bishop of the Personal Ordinariate of the Chair of Saint Peter, who concerning the intersection of accompaniment, discernment, and conscience, offers the following cogent reminder in his 2017 pastoral letter *A Pledged Troth: A Pastoral Letter on Amoris Laetitia*: "Such discernment, which incorporates individual conscience in its reflection, is not, however, a matter for the individual to determine privately, but must be 'guided by the responsible and serious discernment of one's pastor.'"⁶ Are bishops like Lopes not faithfully following an unfortunately commonly overlooked passage in *Amoris Laetitia*? "The thinking of pastors and theologians, if faithful to the Church, honest, realistic, and creative, will help us to achieve greater clarity."⁷ We appreciate the many bishops who have undertaken such transmission of clarity, in light of their healthy exercise of calling the laity to both mercy and repentance in the interest of righteousness.

We likewise appreciate the profound warmth of bishops who care deeply for their flock, as we see for example in the writings of Cardinal Theodore McCarrick, whose 2011 book, *Thinking of You: The Weekly Columns from the Catholic Standard,* show the abiding affection that he maintained for the faithful of the Archdiocese of Washington during his time as archbishop between 2001 and 2006. During this relatively brief span of only five years, Cardinal McCarrick led his flock through the societal tumult that accompanied the jihadist attacks of September 11, 2001, the beginning of

---

5. Arinze, *The Layperson's Distinctive Role*, 75–76.
6. Lopes, *A Pledged Troth*, 12, referencing Francis, *Amoris Laetitia*, 303, 307.
7. Francis, *Amoris Laetitia*, 2.

A Conclusive Message of Gratitude for Our Bishops

the Iraq War in 2003, and the death of John Paul II. Thank you to the many faithful bishops whose personable natures have provided the laity with the presence of a loving spiritual father.

We thank the bishops for leading us when we encounter the numerous other challenges that the twenty-first century continues to present. The genocidal magnitude of abortion, leaving vast numbers of innocent unborn children killed (in the United States alone, on average, at least one in five human lives conceived[8]), and their parents wounded, as well as a pervasive contraceptive mentality and similarly injurious threats to the family, have been waged as an onslaught that leaves many victims in its wake. Thank you to those bishops who have promoted God's vision for chastity, abstinence, and the strong familial bonds forged by the union of husband and wife in holy matrimony, which can continue to be strengthened and highlighted to an even greater extent. The bishops ought to know that the laity remains quite capable of living chastely, but this is made easier with a bishop's prayers and words of support, such as those extended by Cardinal Dolan in the setting of the Synod on the Family in October 2015:

> Can I suggest as well that there is now a *new minority* in the world and even in the Church? I am thinking of those who, relying on God's grace and mercy, strive for virtue and fidelity: Couples who—given the fact that, at least in North America, only half of our people even enter the sacrament of matrimony—approach the Church for the sacrament; couples who, inspired by the Church's teaching that marriage is forever, have persevered through trials; couples who welcome God's gifts of many babies; a young man and woman who have chosen not to live together until marriage; a gay man or woman who wants to be chaste; a couple who has decided that the wife would sacrifice a promising professional career to stay at home and raise their children—these wonderful people today often feel themselves a *minority*, certainly in culture, but even, at times in the Church! I believe there are many more of them than we think, but, given today's pressure,

---

8. National Right to Life Committee, "Abortion Statistics," 2.

they often feel *excluded*. Where do they receive support and encouragement? From TV? From magazines or newspapers? From movies? From Broadway? From their peers? Forget it! They are looking to the Church, and to *us*, for support and encouragement, a warm sense of inclusion. We cannot let them down!"[9]

There are many bishops who have promoted the church's teachings on family life in various ways. We can thus thank bishops such as Cardinal Blase Cupich of the Archdiocese of Chicago, for facilitating—as of July 2016—the opportunity for the staff of the Archdiocese of Chicago to take up to twelve weeks of paid leave following the birth or adoption of a child.[10] The faithful thank those bishops who have supported the health of the family structure in a society more bent on careerism and productivity.

Affronts to religious liberty for Catholics, both internationally as in the Middle East and within the "developed" nations of the West, continue, as does the fallout of the Sexual Revolution and subsequent manifestations of ideological colonization. Pope Francis and his bishops have spoken against this forcefully. Thank you to those multiple bishops who have shown fortitude in defending religious freedom, even when the church's stance on an issue is not deemed popular by broader society.

In terms of other factors, rising anti-Semitism around the globe means that the bishops will have to continue fostering interreligious dialogue in the defense of those of the Jewish faith, as well as those of other faith communities, as we have seen in such writings as the Pontifical Commission for Religious Relations with the Jews' 1998 document, *We Remember: A Reflection on the Shoah*. Along with interreligious dialogue, ecumenism between Catholics and our brother Christians is vital for the bishops to maintain, keeping in mind the progress that has been made over the last century in particular. 2017 marks five hundred years since the beginning of the Protestant Reformation by Martin Luther,

---

9. Dolan, "Inclusion of the New Minority," October 12, 2015.

10. *Chicago Catholic*, "Archdiocese Announces New Parental Leave Policy," May 15–28, 2016.

A Conclusive Message of Gratitude for Our Bishops

and in the midst of this lamentably continued division, we look to the future with hope based on documents such as the Pontifical Council for Promoting Christian Unity and Lutheran World Federation's 2013 collaboration titled, *From Conflict to Communion: Lutheran-Catholic Common Commemoration of the Reformation in 2017*. Thank you to those multiple bishops who have so positively contributed to fomenting good relations between Catholics and other Christians.

On an especially somber note, thank you to those bishops who have labored to foster reconciliation with the victims of the priest sexual abuse scandal, as well as to help the church restore credibility as an institution in a world anxious to offer generalizations against authority, rather than to give credence to the church's endeavors to not let the grave sins of some woefully misguided individuals determine the aspect of the whole. Over the last fifteen years, the bishops have maintained this as a justifiably prime goal.

A special thank you to the bishops of the global south. As was alluded to previously, the future of the church rests significantly in Africa, Latin America, and Asia. The bishops of these areas of the world, typically evangelized during the European colonial era within the last five hundred years, are now tasked with evangelizing other areas around the globe, especially within the West. We saw in the 2014 and 2015 Synod on the Family the increasingly prominent voice that the African bishops maintain within the broader episcopate. A good book to read in this regard is the 2015 book, *Christ's New Homeland—Africa: Contribution to the Synod on the Family by African Pastors*. Note, in his 2015 book, *God or Nothing: A Conversation on Faith with Nicolas Diat*, how Cardinal Robert Sarah of Guinea uses parental imagery to refocus our attention on how the church must promote morality in the interest of drawing us closer to God in the process: "In season and out of season, the Church must recall that life cannot be summed up in terms of the satisfaction of material pleasures, without moral rules. At the end of a journey without God there is only the unhappiness of a child deprived of his parents. Yes, hope abides in God alone!"[11]

---

11. Sarah, *God or Nothing*, 172.

To reiterate what was covered within the chapter on evangelization, in modern times, bishops do well to use the media available, as did Venerable Archbishop Fulton Sheen (further referenced imminently) during his era, to engage and guide their flock heavenward. As one instance of various, Bishop Robert Barron, an auxiliary of the Archdiocese of Los Angeles, has used his media platforms, including his 2016 book, *Vibrant Paradoxes: The Both/And of Catholicism*, to lead his flock lovingly, mercifully, patiently, and ultimately truthfully by revealing to them the manifold considerations that come with presenting the faith accurately to a doubt-ridden world, drawing the church to fathom who Jesus Christ is, who we are subsequently, and what we must always recall about spreading the Good News: "[The Church] should lead today as it led two thousand years ago, with the stunning news that Jesus Christ is the Lord, and the joy of that proclamation should be as evident now as it was then."[12] The possibilities of spreading the Good News via the media available—especially with the convenience and accessibility of social media—are boundless. Thank you to those many bishops who have brought an awareness of Christ to the faithful around the globe by way of mass communications (no pun intended).

A final thank you is extended to those bishops who are constantly and devotedly helping their flock to attain sainthood. Many popes and other bishops throughout the last nearly two millennia have been beatified and ultimately canonized: among the 266 total popes from Peter to Francis, nine have been beatified, and eighty canonized. That rate is not bad, but it could always be higher. Assuredly, the Catholic Church's recognition of these men's personal sanctity is reflected in great part due to their having helped the laity of their time—as well as of today, by extension—on the path to their own daily sanctification during their walk with the Lord. Saint Pius X so famously drew the faithful to more frequent reception of the Eucharist. Saint John Paul II did likewise, reminding us for instance in his 1988 post-synodal apostolic exhortation, *Christifideles Laici: On the Vocation and Mission of the Lay Faithful in the*

---

12. Barron, *Vibrant Paradoxes*, 265.

A Conclusive Message of Gratitude for Our Bishops

Church and in the World, that, "the Bishop in his person has a responsibility towards the lay faithful, in forming the animation and guidance of their Christian life through the proclamation of the Word and the celebration of the Eucharist and the Sacraments."[13] Venerable Fulton Sheen used his gift of written and spoken communication, magnified particularly on mainstream television, to spread the joy that comes with serving Christ. In consideration of Saint Peter, the first pope and therefore the first bishop of bishops, Sheen offered these words in his 1958 book *Life of Christ,* drawing us to recall that Peter was thinking in worldly terms when he thrice denied Jesus, but in heavenly terms when he ultimately offered up his own life rather than to deny him ever again: "Now Peter saw that it was only in the light of the Cross of Calvary that the Cross he would embrace had meaning and significance."[14] As such, thank God that he has gifted us with an era of holy bishops of Rome, with the twentieth century alone featuring the blessings that have stemmed from the pontificates of Saint Pius X, Saint John XXIII, Blessed Paul VI, and Saint John Paul II.

To close this book, let us recall briefly an excerpt from within the Gospels that could easily be neglected if not afforded its proper attention: "At the sight of the crowds, [Jesus'] heart was moved with pity for them, because they were troubled and abandoned, like sheep without a shepherd" (Matt 9:36). The laity thanks you, faithful shepherds, our heroes for the New Evangelization, for leading us faithfully and charitably, ensuring that we are sheep *with* shepherds, with all of our hearts—clergy and laity alike—ideally centered on the Good Shepherd, our Lord and Savior Jesus Christ, in the perpetually enduring interests of the kingdom of God.

---

13. John Paul II, *Christifideles Laici,* 61.
14. Sheen, *Life of Christ,* 429.

About the Author

Justin McClain is a theology and Spanish teacher at his alma mater (class of 2000), Bishop McNamara High School, in Forestville, Maryland, where he has taught since 2006. He has also served as an adjunct instructor of English (as a second language) at Prince George's Community College and adjunct lecturer in Spanish in the "Upward Bound"/Pre-College Programs at the University of Maryland, College Park. Justin holds a B.A. in Spanish Language and Literature (2004) and a B.A. in Criminology and Criminal Justice (2004) from the University of Maryland, College Park, an M.A. in Spanish Language and Culture (2008) from the Universidad de Salamanca (Spain), and an M.A. in International History (2011) from Staffordshire University (England). He has studied philosophy and theology at the undergraduate and graduate levels at the Immaculate Conception Seminary—School of Theology at Seton Hall University and the Franciscan University of Steubenville (where he is currently pursuing a distance learning-based M.A. in theology and Christian ministry), and is studying Church history through the University of Notre Dame's Satellite Theological Education Program. Justin is certified to teach theology by the Archdiocese of Washington, and has provided consultation to the United States Conference of Catholic Bishops' Secretariat of Cultural Diversity in the Church—Subcommittee on

About the Author

African-American Affairs. He has also provided consultation as a theology textbook reviewer, and written for, Ave Maria Press, including his book *Called to Teach: Daily Inspiration for Catholic Educators* (2016, Ave Maria Press). Just has also provided content for Ave Maria Press's *Engaging Faith* blog and high school newsletter. In addition to Justin's work for Ave Maria Press, he has provided publications for the Archdiocese of Atlanta's Office of Black Catholic Ministry, *Aleteia*, the University of Notre Dame McGrath Institute for Church Life's journal *Church Life*, Sophia Institute Press (the *Catholic Exchange* and *EpicPew* websites), the National Catholic Educational Association's *NCEATalk* blog, and *Our Sunday Visitor—Newsweekly*. Justin has also written *Mientras el sol pasaba: Una descripción breve de los rasgos políticos y de los asuntos monárquicos durante la época de Felipe II de España* (2013, Editorial Académica Española) and *Stepping into the Darkness: Post-Holocaust British-American Co-operation in Liberation and Humanitarian Aid to Displaced Populations, 1945–1948* (2012, Lambert Academic Publishing), both of which originated with his master's-level theses. As an advocate for pro-life ministries, Justin serves on the Board of Directors for the Forestville Pregnancy Center in Temple Hills, Maryland. As a life-long Prince Georgian and Marylander, he also serves on the Board of Directors for the Prince George's County Historical Society and is a member of the Maryland Historical Society. Justin, his wife Bernadette, and their children live in Maryland, and are parishioners at Sacred Heart Catholic Church in Bowie.

Bibliography

Archdiocese of Washington. "Cardinal Wuerl Honors More Than 800 Couples Celebrating Milestone Wedding Anniversaries," June 15, 2014. Accessed January 10, 2017. http://adw.org/2014/06/15/cardinal-wuerl-honors-800-couples-celebrating-milestone-wedding-anniversaries/.

Arinze, Francis. *The Layperson's Distinctive Role*. San Francisco: Ignatius, 2013.

———. *Meeting Other Believers: The Risks and Rewards of Interreligious Dialogue*. Huntington: Our Sunday Visitor, 1998.

———. *Religions for Peace: A Call for Solidarity to the Religions of the World*. New York City: Doubleday, 2002.

———, et al. *Christ's New Homeland—Africa: Contribution to the Synod on the Family by African Pastors*. San Francisco: Ignatius, 2015.

Arizona Catholic Conference. *You Welcomed Me: A Pastoral Letter on Migration Released on the Feast of Our Lady of Guadalupe*. Phoenix: 2005. Accessed January 24, 2017. http://dphx.org/wp-content/uploads/2015/09/PL-You-Welcomed-Me-121505.pdf.

Barron, Robert. *Vibrant Paradoxes: The Both/And of Catholicism*. Skokie: Word on Fire, 2016.

Benedict XV. *Spiritus Paraclitus: Encyclical on Saint Jerome*. Vatican City: Libreria Editrice Vaticana, 1920. Accessed January 10, 2017. https://w2.vatican.va/content/benedict-xv/en/encyclicals/documents/hf_ben-xv_enc_15091920_spiritus-paraclitus.html.

Benedict XVI. *Caritatis in Veritate: Encyclical on Integral Human Development in Charity and Truth*. Vatican City: Libreria Editrice Vaticana, 2009. Accessed January 16, 2017. http://w2.vatican.va/content/benedict-xvi/en/encyclicals/documents/hf_ben-xvi_enc_20090629_caritas-in-veritate.html.

———. *Deus Caritas Est: Encyclical on Christian Love*. Vatican City: Libreria Editrice Vaticana, 2005. Accessed January 10, 2017. http://w2.vatican.

Bibliography

va/content/benedict-xvi/en/encyclicals/documents/hf_ben-xvi_enc_20051225_deus-caritas-est.html.

———, as Joseph Ratzinger. *Doctrinal Note on Some Questions Regarding the Participation of Catholics in Political Life*. Vatican City: 2002. Accessed January 12, 2017. http://www.vatican.va/roman_curia/congregations/cfaith/documents/rc_con_cfaith_doc_20021124_politica_en.html.

———. "The Human Person, the Heart of Peace." Message for the World Day of Peace, January 1, 2007. Vatican City: Libreria Editrice Vaticana, 2006. Accessed January 16, 2017. http://w2.vatican.va/content/benedict-xvi/en/messages/peace/documents/hf_ben-xvi_mes_20061208_xl-world-day-peace.html.

———. "Inaugural Pontifical Homily." April 24, 2005. Vatican City: Libreria Editrice Vaticana, 2005. Accessed January 16, 2017. https://w2.vatican.va/content/benedict-xvi/en/homilies/2005/documents/hf_ben-xvi_hom_20050424_inizio-pontificato.html.

———. *The Joy of Knowing Christ: Meditations on the Gospels*. Frederick: The Word Among Us, 2009.

———. "Lecture of the Holy Father: Faith, Reason, and the University—Memories and Reflections." September 12, 2006. Vatican City: Libreria Editrice Vaticana, 2006. Accessed January 18, 2017. http://w2.vatican.va/content/benedict-xvi/en/speeches/2006/september/documents/hf_ben-xvi_spe_20060912_university-regensburg.html.

———. *Saint Paul: Spiritual Thoughts Series*. Washington, DC: USCCB, 2008.

———. *Spe Salvi: Encyclical on Christian Hope*. Vatican City: Libreria Editrice Vaticana, 2007. Accessed January 20, 2017. http://w2.vatican.va/content/benedict-xvi/en/encyclicals/documents/hf_ben-xvi_enc_20071130_spe-salvi.html.

———. *Verbum Domini: Post-Synodal Apostolic Exhortation on the Word of God in the Life and Mission of the Church*. Vatican City: Libreria Editrice Vaticana, 2010. Accessed January 10, 2017. http://w2.vatican.va/content/benedict-xvi/en/apost_exhortations/documents/hf_ben-xvi_exh_20100930_verbum-domini.html.

Bergoglio, Jorge and Abraham Skorka. *On Heaven and Earth—Pope Francis on Faith, Family, and the Church in the Twenty-First Century*. New York City: Image, 2013.

Bransfield, Michael. *Setting Children Free: Loosening the Bonds of Poverty in West Virginia, Pastoral Letter*. Diocese of Wheeling-Charleston: 2012. Accessed February 13, 2017. http://www.dwc.org/files/Pastoral_Letter/28629%20DWC%20pastoral%20letter-REV-11-13-12.pdf.

Blackman, Daniel. "Nigerian Bishop Doeme Combats Boko Haram with 'Rosary Battle Plan.'" In *National Catholic Register*, October 12, 2016. Accessed February 12, 2017. http://www.ncregister.com/daily-news/nigerian-bishop-doeme-combats-boko-haram-with-rosary-battle-plan.

Braxton, Edward. *The Racial Divide in the United States: A Reflection for the World Day of Peace* 2015. Diocese of Belleville: 2015. Accessed February

Bibliography

16, 2017. http://bellevillemessenger.org/2014/12/bishop-braxton-writes-a-letter-on-racial-divide-in-the-united-states/.

Burke, Raymond. *Hope for the World: To Unite All Things in Christ.* San Francisco: Ignatius, 2016.

Canadian Conference of Catholic Bishops. *The Struggle Against Poverty: A Sign of Hope in Our World—Pastoral Letter by the Episcopal Commission for Social Affairs on the Elimination of Poverty.* Ottawa: CCCB, 1996. Accessed February 14, 2017. http://www.cccb.ca/site/eng/media-room/official-texts/pastoral-letters/769-the-struggle-against-poverty-a-sign-of-hope-in-our-world.

Canadian Conference of Catholic Bishops. *We Are Aliens and Transients Before the Lord Our God: A Pastoral Letter on Immigration and the Protection of Refugees.* Ottana: CCCB, 2006. Accessed January 24, 2017. http://www.cccb.ca/site/Files/PastoralLetter_Immigration.html.

———. *"You Love All That Exists . . . All Things Are Yours, God, Lover of Life": A Pastoral Letter on the Christian Ecological Imperative from the Social Affairs Commission, Canadian Conference of Catholic Bishops.* Ottawa: CCCB, 2003. Accessed January 15, 2017. http://www.cccb.ca/site/Files/pastoralenvironment.pdf.

Catechism of the Catholic Church, 2nd ed. Washington, DC: United States Conference of Catholic Bishops, 2000.

Catholic Church and Lutheran World Federation. *Joint Declaration on the Doctrine of Justification.* Vatican City: 1999. Accessed January 18, 2017. http://www.vatican.va/roman_curia/pontifical_councils/chrstuni/documents/rc_pc_chrstuni_doc_31101999_cath-luth-joint-declaration_en.html.

Catholic Bishops of England and Wales. *The Call, the Journey, and the Mission: An Invitation from the Bishops of England and Wales to Reflect on the Gift of Marriage and Family Life.* Diocese of Birmingham, UK: 2014. Accessed January 10, 2017. http://www.birminghamdiocese.org.uk/wp-content/uploads/2014/12/The-Call-Journey-Mission-of-the-Family-Pastoral-Letter-pdf.pdf.

Catholic News Agency. "Vatican Announces Plans to Become First 'Carbon Neutral State' in the World." July 13, 2007. Accessed January 16, 2017. http://www.catholicnewsagency.com/news/vatican_announces_plans_to_become_first_carbon_neutral_state_in_the_world/.

Center for Applied Research in the Apostolate. "Frequently Requested Church Statistics." Washington, DC: Georgetown University, 2016. Accessed January 3, 2017. http://cara.georgetown.edu/frequently-requested-church-statistics/.

Chaput, Charles. *Equipping Saints: A Pastoral Letter on Catholic Education and Faith Formation.* Archdiocese of Philadelphia: 2014. Accessed January 9, 2017. http://archphila.org/archbishop-chaput/statements/COA-EquippingSaints2014.pdf.

———. *Render unto Caesar: Serving the Nation by Living Our Catholic Beliefs in Political Life.* New York City: Doubleday, 2008.

Bibliography

———. "There Is No Equivalence," *Catholic Philly*, August 10, 2015. Accessed February 18, 2017. http://catholicphilly.com/2015/08/think-tank/archbishop-chaput-column/there-is-no-equivalence/.

Clarke, Kevin. "Health Care Disunity Revisited in George's USCCB Address," *America: The Jesuit Review*, November 15, 2010. Accessed March 5, 2017. http://www.americamagazine.org/content/all-things/health-care-disunity-revisited-georges-usccb-address.

Congregation for the Doctrine of the Faith. *Dominus Iesus: Declaration on the Unicity and Salvific Universality of Jesus Christ and the Church*. Vatican City: 2000. Accessed January 18, 2017. http://www.vatican.va/roman_curia/congregations/cfaith/documents/rc_con_cfaith_doc_20000806_dominus-iesus_en.html.

———. *Educational Guidance on Human Love: Outlines for Sex Education*. Vatican City: 1983. Accessed January 22, 2017. http://www.vatican.va/roman_curia/congregations/ccatheduc/documents/rc_con_ccatheduc_doc_19831101_sexual-education_en.html.

———. *Letter to the Bishops of the Catholic Church on the Pastoral Care of Homosexual Persons*. Vatican City: 1986. Accessed January 22, 2017. http://www.vatican.va/roman_curia/congregations/cfaith/documents/rc_con_cfaith_doc_19861001_homosexual-persons_en.html.

———. *Persona Humana: Declaration on Certain Questions Concerning Sexual Ethics*. Vatican City: 1975. Accessed January 22, 2017. http://www.vatican.va/roman_curia/congregations/cfaith/documents/rc_con_cfaith_doc_19751229_persona-humana_en.html.

Cordileone, Salvatore. "Married Love and the Transformation of the Human by the Divine." Homily. Archdiocese of San Francisco: 2015. Accessed January 10, 2017. https://sfarchdiocese.org/docs/default-source/archbishop-office/archbishop's-homilies/married-love-and-the-transformation-of-the-human-by-the-divined3f2053b401d6473b6e2ff0000a14dof.pdf?sfvrsn=0.

DiMarzio, Nicholas. *Brothers and Sisters in Christ: A Catholic Teaching on the Issue of Immigration*. Irving: Basilica, 2008.

Dolan, Timothy. "Inclusion of the New Minority." October 12, 2015. Archdiocese of New York. Accessed February 22, 2017. http://cardinaldolan.org/index.php/inclusion-of-the-new-minority/.

Duriga, Joyce. "Archdiocese Announces New Parental Leave Policy." In *Chicago Catholic*, May 15–28, 2016. Archdiocese of Chicago. Accessed February 22, 2017. http://www.chicagocatholic.com/cnwonline/2016/0515/2.aspx.

Egan, Philip. *The Future of Our Catholic Schools, Pastoral Letter*. Diocese of Portsmouth: 2016. Accessed January 10, 2017. http://www.portsmouthdiocese.org.uk/bishop/pastoral_letters/20161002-BoP-PL-Catholic-Schools-A5.pdf.

Francis. "Address of the Holy Father—Meeting with the Members of the General Assembly of the United Nations Organization." September 25, 2015. Vatican City: Libreria Editrice Vaticana, 2015. Accessed January

22, 2017. http://w2.vatican.va/content/francesco/en/speeches/2015/september/documents/papa-francesco_20150925_onu-visita.html.

———. "Address to the Plenary Session of the Pontifical Academy of Sciences on the Occasion of the Inauguration of the Bust in Honor of Pope Benedict XVI." October 27, 2014. Vatican City: Libreria Editrice Vaticana, 2014. Accessed January 16, 2017. https://w2.vatican.va/content/francesco/en/speeches/2014/october/documents/papa-francesco_20141027_plenaria-accademia-scienze.html.

———. *Amoris Laetitia: On Love in the Family, Apostolic Exhortation*. Vatican City: Libreria Editrice Vaticana, 2016. Accessed January 22, 2017. http://w2.vatican.va/content/dam/francesco/pdf/apost_exhortations/documents/papa-francesco_esortazione-ap_20160319_amoris-laetitia_en.pdf.

———. "Dialogue of the Holy Father with the Bishops of Poland—Response to Bishop Krzysztof Zadarko." July 27, 2016. Vatican City: 2016. Accessed January 22, 2017. http://press.vatican.va/content/salastampa/it/bollettino/pubblico/2016/08/02/0568/01265.html#en.

———. *Evangelii Gaudium: On the Proclamation of the Gospel in Today's World, Apostolic Exhortation*. Vatican City: Libreria Editrice Vaticana, 2013. Accessed January 20, 2017. https://w2.vatican.va/content/francesco/en/apost_exhortations/documents/papa-francesco_esortazione-ap_20131124_evangelii-gaudium.html.

———. *Laudato Si': Encyclical on Care for Our Common Home*. Vatican City: Libreria Editrice Vaticana, 2015. Accessed January 16, 2017. http://w2.vatican.va/content/francesco/en/encyclicals/documents/papa-francesco_20150524_enciclica-laudato-si.html.

———. *Lumen Fidei: Encyclical on the Light of Faith*. Vatican City: Libreria Editrice Vaticana, 2013. Accessed January 10, 2017. http://w2.vatican.va/content/francesco/en/encyclicals/documents/papa-francesco_20130629_enciclica-lumen-fidei.html.

———, and Kirill. *Joint Declaration of Pope Francis and Patriarch Kirill of Moscow and All Russia*. Vatican City: Libreria Editrice Vaticana, 2016. Accessed January 18, 2017. https://w2.vatican.va/content/francesco/en/speeches/2016/february/documents/papa-francesco_20160212_dichiarazione-comune-kirill.html#Joint_Declaration.

George, Francis. *The Difference God Makes: A Catholic Vision of Faith, Communion, and Culture*. New York City: Crossroad, 2009.

——— *God in Action: How Faith in God Can Address the Challenges of the World*. New York City: Doubleday, 2011.

Gómez, José. *Immigration and the Next America: Renewing the Soul of Our Nation*. Huntington: Our Sunday Visitor, 2013.

———. *Men of Brave Heart: The Virtue of Courage in the Priestly Life*. Huntington: Our Sunday Visitor, 2009.

Harmon, Catherine. "Cardinals Kasper and Dolan and the African Bishops: Two Interviews, Two Different Takes." In *Catholic World Report*, October 15,

2014. Accessed February 18, 2017. http://www.catholicworldreport.com/Blog/3437/cardinals_kasper_and_dolan_and_the_african_bishops.aspx.

Holdren, Alan. "Pope Francis Warns West Over 'Ideological Colonization.'" In *National Catholic Register*, January 20, 2015. Accessed January 22, 2017. http://www.ncregister.com/daily-news/pope-francis-warns-west-over-ideological-colonization.

Jeanbart, Jean-Clement. "Letter to Carl Anderson and the Knights of Columbus." May 27, 2015. Archdiocese of Aleppo, Syria. Accessed February 12, 2017. http://www.kofc.org/en/resources/charities/christian-relief/archbishop-jeanbart-letter.pdf.

John XXIII. *Mater et Magistra: Encyclical on Christianity and Social Progress*. Vatican City: Libreria Editrice Vaticana, 1961. Accessed February 14, 2017. http://w2.vatican.va/content/john-xxiii/en/encyclicals/documents/hf_j-xxiii_enc_15051961_mater.html.

———. *Pacem in Terris: Encyclical on Establishing Universal Peace in Truth, Justice, Charity, and Liberty*. Vatican City: Libreria Editrice Vaticana, 1963. Accessed February 22, 2017. http://w2.vatican.va/content/john-xxiii/en/encyclicals/documents/hf_j-xxiii_enc_11041963_pacem.html.

John Paul II. *Christifideles Laici: On the Vocation and the Mission of the Lay Faithful in the Church and in the World, Post-Synodal Apostolic Exhortation*. Vatican City: Libreria Editrice Vaticana, 1988. Accessed February 22, 2017. http://w2.vatican.va/content/john-paul-ii/en/apost_exhortations/documents/hf_jp-ii_exh_30121988_christifideles-laici.html.

———. *Ecclesia de Eucharistia: Encyclical on the Eucharist and Its Relationship to the Church*. Vatican City: 2003. Accessed February 22, 2017. http://www.vatican.va/holy_father/special_features/encyclicals/documents/hf_jp-ii_enc_20030417_ecclesia_eucharistia_en.html.

———. *Ecclesia in Africa: On the Church in Africa and Its Evangelizing Mission Towards the Year 2000, Post-Synodal Apostolic Exhortation*. Vatican City: Libreria Editrice Vaticana, 1995. Accessed January 26, 2017. http://w2.vatican.va/content/john-paul-ii/en/apost_exhortations/documents/hf_jp-ii_exh_14091995_ecclesia-in-africa.html.

———. *Ecclesia in America: On the Encounter with the Living Jesus Christ—The Way to Conversion, Communion, and Solidarity in America, Post-Synodal Apostolic Exhortation*. Vatican City: Libreria Editrice Vaticana, 1999. Accessed January 19, 2017. http://w2.vatican.va/content/john-paul-ii/en/apost_exhortations/documents/hf_jp-ii_exh_22011999_ecclesia-in-america.html.

———. *Ecclesia in Asia: On Jesus Christ the Savior and His Mission of Love and Service in Asia—" . . . That They May Have Life, and Have It Abundantly (John 10:10)" Post-Synodal Apostolic Exhortation*. Vatican City: Libreria Editrice Vaticana, 1999. Accessed January 26, 2017. http://w2.vatican.va/content/john-paul-ii/en/apost_exhortations/documents/hf_jp-ii_exh_06111999_ecclesia-in-asia.html.

Bibliography

———. *Ex Corde Ecclesiae: Apostolic Constitution on Catholic Universities.* Vatican City: Libreria Editrice Vaticana, 1990. Accessed January 9, 2017. http://w2.vatican.va/content/john-paul-ii/en/apost_constitutions/documents/hf_jp-ii_apc_15081990_ex-corde-ecclesiae.html.

———. *Familiaris Consortio: Post-Synodal Apostolic Exhortation on the Role of the Christian Family in the Modern World.* Vatican City: Libreria Editrice Vaticana, 1981. Accessed January 12, 2017. http://w2.vatican.va/content/john-paul-ii/en/apost_exhortations/documents/hf_jp-ii_exh_19811122_familiaris-consortio.html.

———. *Fides et Ratio: Encyclical on the Relationship Between Faith and Reason.* Vatican City: Libreria Editrice Vaticana, 1998. Accessed January 6, 2017. http://w2.vatican.va/content/john-paul-ii/en/encyclicals/documents/hf_jp-ii_enc_14091998_fides-et-ratio.html.

———. *Gift and Mystery: On the Fiftieth Anniversary of My Priestly Ordination.* New York City: Image, 1996.

———. *Love and Responsibility.* San Francisco: Ignatius, 1993.

———. "Message to the Pontifical Academy of Sciences: On Evolution." October 22, 1996. Vatican City: Libreria Editrice Vaticana, 1996. Accessed January 16, 2017. https://w2.vatican.va/content/john-paul-ii/it/messages/pont_messages/1996/documents/hf_jp-ii_mes_19961022_evoluzione.html.

———. *Mulieris Dignitatem: Apostolic Letter on the Dignity and Vocation of Women on the Occasion of the Marian Year.* Vatican City: Libreria Editrice Vaticana, 1988. Accessed January 22, 2017. https://w2.vatican.va/content/john-paul-ii/en/apost_letters/1988/documents/hf_jp-ii_apl_19880815_mulieris-dignitatem.html.

———. "Peace with God the Creator, Peace with All of Creation." In *Message for the World Day of Peace*, January 1, 1990. Vatican City: Libreria Editrice Vaticana, 1989. Accessed January 14, 2017. http://w2.vatican.va/content/john-paul-ii/en/messages/peace/documents/hf_jp-ii_mes_19891208_xxiii-world-day-for-peace.html.

———. *Ut Unum Sint: Encyclical on Commitment to Ecumenism.* Vatican City: Libreria Editrice Vaticana, 1995. Accessed January 17, 2017. http://w2.vatican.va/content/john-paul-ii/en/encyclicals/documents/hf_jp-ii_enc_25051995_ut-unum-sint.html.

Knights of Columbus. "Knights of Columbus Provides Major Report on Genocide of Christians to State Department." March 10, 2016. Accessed February 12, 2017. http://www.kofc.org/en/news/media/kofc-provides-major-report-genocide-ma.html.

Leo XIII. *Providentissimus Deus: Encyclical on the Study of Holy Scripture.* Vatican City: Libreria Editrice Vaticana, 1893. Accessed January 10, 2017. http://w2.vatican.va/content/leo-xiii/en/encyclicals/documents/hf_l-xiii_enc_18111893_providentissimus-deus.html.

———. *Rerum Novarum: Encyclical on Capital and Labor.* Vatican City: Libreria Editrice Vaticana, 1891. Accessed February 13, 2017. http://w2.vatican.

Bibliography

va/content/leo-xiii/en/encyclicals/documents/hf_l-xiii_enc_15051891_rerum-novarum.html.

Lopes, Steven. *A Pledged Troth: A Pastoral Letter on Amoris Laetitia*. Houston: The Personal Ordinariate of the Chair of Saint Peter, 2017.

Lori, William. *The Joy of Believing: A Practical Guide to the Catholic Faith*. Frederick: The Word Among Us, 2015.

Loverde, Paul. *Bought with a Price: Every Man's Duty to Protect Himself and His Family from Pornographic Culture*. Diocese of Arlington: 2014. Accessed January 22, 2017. https://www.arlingtondiocese.org/uploadedFiles/Library/docs/Communications/Letters_from_Bishop_Loverde/Bought_with_a_Price.pdf.

Maryland Catholic Conference. *Comfort and Consolation: Care of the Sick and Dying—A Pastoral Letter from the Catholic Bishops of Maryland*. Annapolis: 2014. Accessed February 19, 2017. http://www.mdcathcon.org/library/public/Documents/Publications/14C-C-Final-small.pdf.

McCarrick, Theodore. *Thinking of You: The Weekly Columns from the Catholic Standard*. Notre Dame: Ave Maria, 2011.

Melczek, Dale. *Created in God's Image: A Pastoral Letter on the Sin of Racism and a Call to Conversion*. Diocese of Gary: 2003. Accessed February 16, 2017. http://www.dcgary.org/pdf/Created-In-Gods-Image.pdf.

Missika, Jean-Louis and Dominique Wolton. *Choosing God—Chosen by God: Conversations with Jean-Marie Lustiger*. San Francisco: Ignatius, 1991.

Murry, George. *Who Is My Neighbor?: A Pastoral Letter on the Occasion of National Poverty Awareness Month*. Diocese of Youngstown: 2012. Accessed February 13, 2017. http://doy.org/images/PDF/Bishop%20Murrys%20Pastoral%20Letter%20on%20Poverty.pdf.

National Right to Life Committee. "Abortion Statistics: United States Data and Trends." Accessed February 23, 2017. http://www.nrlc.org/uploads/factsheets/FS01AbortionintheUS.pdf.

New American Bible. Revised Edition. Washington, DC: United States Conference of Catholic Bishops, 2011.

Niederauer, George. *Precious as Silver: Imagining Your Life with God*. Notre Dame: Ave Maria, 2004.

Olmsted, Thomas. *Into the Breach: An Apostolic Exhortation to Catholic Men*. Diocese of Phoenix: 2015. Accessed January 22, 2017. http://www.kofc.org/un/en/resources/college/into-the-breach.pdf.

Paul VI. *Ad Gentes: Decree on the Mission Activity of the Church*. Vatican City: 1965. Accessed January 26, 2017. http://www.vatican.va/archive/hist_councils/ii_vatican_council/documents/vat-ii_decree_19651207_ad-gentes_en.html.

———. *Apostolicam Actuositatem: Decree on the Apostolate of the Laity*. Vatican City: 1965. Accessed February 8, 2017. http://www.vatican.va/archive/hist_councils/ii_vatican_council/documents/vat-ii_decree_19651118_apostolicam-actuositatem_en.html.

Bibliography

———. *Christus Dominus: Decree Concerning the Pastoral Office of Bishops in the Church.* Vatican City: 1965. Accessed January 7, 2017. http://www.vatican.va/archive/hist_councils/ii_vatican_council/documents/vat-ii_decree_19651028_christus-dominus_en.html.

———. *Dei Verbum: Dogmatic Constitution on Divine Revelation.* Vatican City: 1965. Accessed January 10, 2017. http://www.vatican.va/archive/hist_councils/ii_vatican_council/documents/vat-ii_const_19651118_dei-verbum_en.html.

———. *Gaudium et Spes: Pastoral Constitution on the Church in the Modern World.* Vatican City: 1965. Accessed February 7, 2017. http://www.vatican.va/archive/hist_councils/ii_vatican_council/documents/vat-ii_const_19651207_gaudium-et-spes_en.html.

———. *Gravissimum Educationis: Declaration on Christian Education.* Vatican City: 1965. Accessed January 9, 2017. http://www.vatican.va/archive/hist_councils/ii_vatican_council/documents/vat-ii_decl_19651028_gravissimum-educationis_en.html.

———. *Humanae Vitae: Encyclical on the Regulation of Birth.* Vatican City: Libreria Editrice Vaticana, 1968. Accessed January 22, 2017. http://w2.vatican.va/content/paul-vi/en/encyclicals/documents/hf_p-vi_enc_25071968_humanae-vitae.html.

———. *Inter Mirifica: Decree on the Media of Social Communications.* Vatican City: 1963. Accessed February 22, 2017. http://www.vatican.va/archive/hist_councils/ii_vatican_council/documents/vat-ii_decree_19631204_inter-mirifica_en.html.

———. *Lumen Gentium: Dogmatic Constitution on the Church.* Vatican City: 1964. Accessed January 8, 2017. http://www.vatican.va/archive/hist_councils/ii_vatican_council/documents/vat-ii_const_19641121_lumen-gentium_en.html.

———. *Nostra Aetate: Declaration on the Relation of the Church to Non-Christian Religions.* Vatican City: 1965. Accessed January 17, 2017. http://www.vatican.va/archive/hist_councils/ii_vatican_council/documents/vat-ii_decl_19651028_nostra-aetate_en.html.

———. *Populorum Progressio: Encyclical on the Development of Peoples.* Vatican City: Libreria Editrice Vaticana, 1967. Accessed February 14, 2017. http://w2.vatican.va/content/paul-vi/en/encyclicals/documents/hf_p-vi_enc_26031967_populorum.html.

———. *Unitatis Redintegratio: Decree on Ecumenism.* Vatican City: 1964. Accessed January 17, 2017. http://www.vatican.va/archive/hist_councils/ii_vatican_council/documents/vat-ii_decree_19641121_unitatis-redintegratio_en.html.

Pius XI. *Divini Redemptoris: Encyclical on Atheistic Communism.* Vatican City: 1937. Accessed January 11, 2017. http://papalencyclicals.net/Pius11/P11DIVIN.HTM.

———. *Mit Brennender Sorge: Encyclical on the Church and the Third Reich.* Vatican City: Libreria Editrice Vaticana, 1937. Accessed January 11, 2017.

Bibliography

      http://w2.vatican.va/content/pius-xi/en/encyclicals/documents/hf_p-xi_enc_14031937_mit-brennender-sorge.html.

———. *Non Abbiamo Bisogno: Encyclical on Catholic Action in Italy*. Vatican City: Libreria Editrice Vaticana, 1931. Accessed January 11, 2017. http://w2.vatican.va/content/pius-xi/en/encyclicals/documents/hf_p-xi_enc_29061931_non-abbiamo-bisogno.html.

Pius XII. *Divino Afflante Spiritu: Encyclical on Promoting Biblical Studies, Commemorating the Fiftieth Anniversary of Providentissimus Deus*. Vatican City: Libreria Editrice Vaticana, 1943. Accessed January 10, 2017. http://w2.vatican.va/content/pius-xii/en/encyclicals/documents/hf_p-xii_enc_30091943_divino-afflante-spiritu.html.

Pontifical Biblical Commission. *The Historicity of the Gospels*. Vatican City: 1964. Accessed January 10, 2017. http://www.vatican.va/roman_curia/congregations/cfaith/pcb_doc_index.htm.

Pontifical Commission for Religious Relations with the Jews. *We Remember: A Reflection on the Shoah*. Vatican City: 1998. Accessed February 22, 2017. http://www.vatican.va/roman_curia/pontifical_councils/chrstuni/documents/rc_pc_chrstuni_doc_16031998_shoah_en.html.

Pontifical Council for the Family. *The Truth and Meaning of Human Sexuality: Guidelines for Education within the Family*. Vatican City: 1995. Accessed January 22, 2017. http://www.vatican.va/roman_curia/pontifical_councils/family/documents/rc_pc_family_doc_08121995_human-sexuality_en.html.

Pontifical Council for Interreligious Dialogue. *Dialogue in Truth and Charity: Pastoral Orientations for Interreligious Dialogue*. Vatican City: Libreria Editrice Vaticana, 2014. Accessed January 18, 2017. http://www.pcinterreligious.org/uploads/pdfs/DIALOGUE_IN_TRUTH_AND_CHARITY_website-1.pdf.

Pontifical Council for Justice and Peace. *Compendium of the Social Doctrine of the Church*. Vatican City: Libreria Editrice Vaticana, 2005. Accessed February 14, 2017. http://www.vatican.va/roman_curia/pontifical_councils/justpeace/documents/rc_pc_justpeace_doc_20060526_compendio-dott-soc_en.html.

Pontifical Council for Promoting Christian Unity and Lutheran World Federation. *From Conflict to Communion: Lutheran-Catholic Common Commemoration of the Reformation in 2017*. Vatican City: 2013. Accessed February 22, 2017. http://www.vatican.va/roman_curia/pontifical_councils/chrstuni/lutheran-fed-docs/rc_pc_chrstuni_doc_2013_dal-conflitto-alla-comunione_en.html.

Rhoades, Kevin. "Voting from a Catholic Perspective." October 26, 2016. Diocese of Fort Wayne–South Bend. Accessed March 7, 2017. http://www.diocesefwsb.org/Bishop-Rhoades-homilies-and-talks.

Sarah, Robert. *God or Nothing: A Conversation on Faith with Nicolas Diat*. San Francisco: Ignatius, 2016.

Sheen, Fulton. *Life of Christ*. New York City: Image, 1958.

---. *Three to Get Married: An Inspiring Guide to Love and Marriage*. New York City: Dell, 1951.

Tagle, Luis Antonio. *Telling the Story of Jesus: Word—Communion—Mission*. Collegeville: Liturgical, 2015.

United States Conference of Catholic Bishops. *Brothers and Sisters to Us: Pastoral Letter on Racism*. Washington, DC: 1979. Accessed February 16, 2017. http://www.usccb.org/issues-and-action/cultural-diversity/african-american/brothers-and-sisters-to-us.cfm.

---. *The Challenge of Peace: God's Promise and our Response*. Washington, DC: National Conference of Catholic Bishops, 1983.

---. *Create in Me a Clean Heart: A Pastoral Response to Pornography*. Washington, DC: 2015. Accessed January 22, 2017. http://www.usccb.org/issues-and-action/human-life-and-dignity/pornography/upload/Create-in-Me-a-Clean-Heart-Statement-on-Pornography.pdf.

---. *Economic Justice for All: Pastoral Letter on Catholic Social Teaching and the U.S. Economy*. Washington, DC: 1986. Accessed February 13, 2017. http://www.usccb.org/upload/economic_justice_for_all.pdf.

---. *Forming Consciences for Faithful Citizenship: A Call to Political Responsibility from the Catholic Bishops of the United States, with Introductory Note*. Washington, DC: 2015. Accessed January 13, 2017. http://www.usccb.org/issues-and-action/faithful-citizenship/upload/forming-consciences-for-faithful-citizenship.pdf.

---. *Global Climate Change: A Plea for Dialogue, Prudence, and the Common Good, Pastoral Statement*. Washington, DC: 2001. Accessed January 15, 2017. http://www.usccb.org/issues-and-action/human-life-and-dignity/environment/global-climate-change-a-plea-for-dialogue-prudence-and-the-common-good.cfm.

---. *Human Sexuality: A Catholic Perspective for Education and Lifelong Learning*. Washington, DC: United States Catholic Conference, 1990.

---. *Living the Gospel of Life: A Challenge to American Catholics—A Statement by the Catholic Bishops of the United States*. Washington, DC: 1998. Accessed February 18, 2017. http://www.usccb.org/issues-and-action/human-life-and-dignity/abortion/living-the-gospel-of-life.cfm.

---. *On Embryonic Stem Cell Research: A Statement of the United States Conference of Catholic Bishops*. Washington, DC: 2008. Accessed February 18, 2017. http://www.usccb.org/about/pro-life-activities/respect-life-program/upload/On-Embryonic-Stem-Cell-Research.pdf.

---. *Renewing the Earth: An Invitation to Reflection and Action on Environment in Light of Catholic Social Teaching, Pastoral Statement*. Washington, DC: United States Catholic Conference, 1991. Accessed January 14, 2017. http://www.usccb.org/issues-and-action/human-life-and-dignity/environment/renewing-the-earth.cfm.

---. *To Live Each Day with Dignity: A Statement on Physician-Assisted Suicide*. Washington, DC: 2011. Accessed February 19, 2017. http://www.

usccb.org/issues-and-action/human-life-and-dignity/assisted-suicide/to-live-each-day/upload/to-live-each-day-with-dignity-hyperlinked.pdf.

———. *Welcoming the Stranger Among Us: Unity in Diversity*. Washington, DC: United States Catholic Conference, 2000. Accessed January 24, 2017. http://www.usccb.org/issues-and-action/cultural-diversity/pastoral-care-of-migrants-refugees-and-travelers/resources/welcoming-the-stranger-among-us-unity-in-diversity.cfm.

——— and Mexican Bishops' Conference. *Strangers No Longer: Together on the Journey of Hope*. Washington, DC: 2003. Accessed January 24, 2017. http://www.usccb.org/issues-and-action/human-life-and-dignity/immigration/strangers-no-longer-together-on-the-journey-of-hope.cfm.

United States Conference of Catholic Bishops—Ad Hoc Committee for Religious Liberty. *Witnesses to Freedom: Little Sisters of the Poor*. Washington, DC: 2016. Accessed January 12, 2017. http://www.usccb.org/issues-and-action/religious-liberty/fortnight-for-freedom/upload/Little-Sisters-of-the-Poor-Fortnight-2016.pdf.

United States Conference of Catholic Bishops—Committee for Ecumenical and Interreligious Affairs and Evangelical Lutheran Church in America. *Declaration on the Way: Church, Ministry, and Eucharist*. Washington, DC: 2015. Accessed January 18, 2017. http://www.usccb.org/beliefs-and-teachings/ecumenical-and-interreligious/ecumenical/lutheran/upload/Declaration_on_the_Way-for-Website.pdf.

United States Conference of Catholic Bishops—Committee on African-American Catholics. *Love Thy Neighbor as Thyself: U.S. Catholic Bishops Speak Against Racism*. Washington, DC: United States Catholic Conference, 2000.

United States Conference of Catholic Bishops—Committee on Laity, Marriage, Family Life, and Youth. *Marriage: Love and Life in the Divine Plan, Pastoral Letter*. Washington, DC: 2009. Accessed January 10, 2017. http://www.usccb.org/issues-and-action/marriage-and-family/marriage/love-and-life/upload/pastoral-letter-marriage-love-and-life-in-the-divine-plan.pdf.

Vatican Radio. "Pope: Marriage Between Man and Woman, No to Gender Ideology." June 8, 2015. Accessed January 22, 2017. http://en.radiovaticana.va/news/2015/06/08/pope_marriage_between_man_and_woman,_no_to_gender_ideology/1150051.

———. "Nigerian Catholic Bishops: Good Families Make Good Nations." February 26, 2015. Accessed January 10, 2017. http://en.radiovaticana.va/news/2015/02/26/nigerian_catholic_bishops_good_families_make_good_nations/1125751.

———. "Pope Francis: Marriage and the Family Are in Crisis." November 11, 2014. Accessed January 22, 2017. http://en.radiovaticana.va/news/2014/11/17/pope_francis_marriage_and_the_family_are_in_crisis/1111371.

Warda, Bashar Matti. "Letter to Carl Anderson and the Knights of Columbus." May 8, 2015. Chaldean Archdiocese of Erbil, Iraq. Accessed February 12,

Bibliography

2017. http://www.kofc.org/en/resources/charities/christian-relief/bishop-warda-letter.pdf.

Williams, Thomas, ed. *Pope John Paul II: Springtime of Evangelization—The Complete Texts of the Holy Father's 1998 ad Limina Addresses to the Bishops of the United States*. Rancho Santa Fe: Basilica, 1999.

Wooden, Cindy. "Pope Francis and Orthodox Leaders Call on International Community to Respond to Refugee Crisis." In *Catholic Herald*, April 18, 2016. Accessed January 24, 2017. http://www.catholicherald.co.uk/news/2016/04/18/pope-francis-and-orthodox-leaders-call-on-international-community-to-respond-to-refugee-crisis/.

Wuerl, Donald. *Catholic Education: Looking to the Future with Confidence, Pastoral Letter*. Archdiocese of Washington: 2008. Accessed January 9, 2017. http://adw.org/wp-content/uploads/2014/02/2008-Education-Pastoral-Letter1.pdf.

———. *The Catholic Way*. New York City: Doubleday, 2001.

———. *Disciples of the Lord: Sharing the Vision—A Pastoral Letter on the New Evangelization*. Archdiocese of Washington: 2010. Accessed January 19, 2017. http://adw.org/wp-content/uploads/2014/02/Disciples-of-the-Lord.pdf.

———. *Faith that Transforms Us: Reflections on the Creed*. Frederick: The Word Among Us, 2013.

———. *New Evangelization: Passing on the Catholic Faith Today*. Huntington: Our Sunday Visitor, 2013.

———. *Seek First the Kingdom: Challenging the Culture by Living Our Faith*. Huntington: Our Sunday Visitor, 2011.

———. *To the Martyrs: A Reflection on the Supreme Christian Witness*. Steubenville: Emmaus Road, 2015.

Zimmermann, Mark. "A Prayer, and a Life, for Justice." August 14, 2013. Accessed January 12, 2017. http://www.cathstan.org/Content/News/Archdiocese/Article/A-prayer-and-a-life-for-justice/2/27/5770.